Data Structures
Practice Problems
for C++ Beginners

Kung-Hua Chang

Table of Contents

Preface

The first few practice problems were developed when I was a Ph.D. student in UCLA fulfilling my TA requirements in Winter 2015. The encouraging feedbacks from students have helped me to improve the practice problems while also retiring inadequate ones. After I received my Ph.D. in Computer Science, I had been a lecturer in UCLA teaching CS 32 about data structures in C++ over the summer of 2015 and 2016. The teaching experiences have contributed to improving some practice problems. Finally, after I finished teaching the summer session in 2016, I had spent a couple months of evenings and weekends revising many of the practice problems (while also adding new practice problems) in order to publish a book to help any students in this subject.

I believe that by providing simple practice problems, students can quickly grasp the concept of the principles of Object-Oriented Programming, Linked Lists, Stacks, Queues, Recursion, Trees, Graphs, Hash Tables, Algorithmic Efficiency, Sorting Algorithms, Heaps, and Generic Programming with C++ STL and Templates as sometimes many examples in a standard data structure textbook may be too complicated for C++ beginners to grasp the important concepts behind them.

This book shall be treated as supplemental materials in addition to a formal introductory C++ book in data structures such as *Data Abstraction and Problem Solving with C++* or the PowerPoint slides (http://careynachenberg.weebly.com/cs-slides.html) from Professor Carey Nachenberg from UCLA. This book should also be helpful to people who just started to learn the principles of object-oriented programming, fundamental data structures, and generic programming (not intended for intermediate / experienced programmers though).

The practice examples in this book should **not** be viewed as examples of good coding styles. The practice examples were sometimes made with the intention to mislead novice programmers by utilizing bad coding styles or programming logic. The practice examples in this book are based on C++03 with some syntax from C++11. All the practice examples should be compiled successfully using Visual C++ 2015, and GCC 4.8.4. Some selected example codes can be found at: https://github.com/KHC999/CS32

Finally, the author hopes to use the proceeds from the sales of this book to establish a scholarship fund in UCLA.

Acknowledgements

I'd like to appreciate Professor David Smallberg from UCLA for his guidance on how to be a better lecturer and Professor Carey Nachenberg for his PowerPoint slides in this subject as well as for his guidance on how to be a better public speaker. I'd also like to give my special thanks to Dr. Josiah L. Carlson for providing book title ideas.

Kung-Hua Chang, Ph.D.

ISBN-13: 978-0-9985440-1-4
ISBN-10: 0998544019

For information about this book, please visit www.simpleandexample.com. If you have any questions regarding this book, please contact simpleandexample@gmail.com

Practice 1 – Data Abstraction and Resource Management

Problem #1.1: If the following program doesn't compile, why not? If it does compile, what is the output when it is run?

```cpp
#include <iostream>
#include <string>
using namespace std;

class A
{
    string str;
};
class B
{
    public:
        B() {      a.str = "hello";     }
        void output() {      cout << a.str << endl;     }
    private:
        A a;
};
int main()
{
    B b;
    b.output();
}
```

Problem #1.2: What is the output of the following program?

```cpp
#include <iostream>
using namespace std;

class Double
{
public:
    Double(): value(0) { cout << "1"; }
    Double(double num): value(num) { cout << "4"; }
    double getValue() { return value; }
    ~Double() { cout << "9"; }
private:
    double value;
};

int main()
{
    Double a,b = 2,c = b;
    a = b;
    cout << a.getValue() << b.getValue() << c.getValue();
}
```

```cpp
#include <iostream>
using namespace std;
class A
{
public:
    A() { cout << "C"; }
    ~A() { cout << "2"; }
};
class B
{
public:
    B() { cout << "S"; }
    ~B() { cout << "3"; }
private:
    A a;
};
int main()
{
    B b;
}
```

```cpp
#include <iostream>
#include <string>
using namespace std;
class student
{
public:
    student(const string &name, const double &score) {
        this->name = name;
        this->score = score;
    }
    void output() {
        cout << "Student's name is: " << name << endl;
        cout << "Score is : " << score << endl;
    }
private:
    string name;
    double score;
};
int main()
{
    student s;      // Hmmm....
    s.output();
}
```

Problem #1.5: The following program will crash when it is run. Please help fix it.

```cpp
#include <iostream>
using namespace std;

class ABC
{
public:
    ABC() { cout << "1"; }
    ~ABC() { cout << "2"; }
};

int main()
{
    ABC *p = new ABC[3];
    delete p;
}
```

Problem #1.6: Please fix the program so that it can print out the following outputs:
T1
T1
5
T1
T1
T1

```cpp
#include <iostream>
using namespace std;

class Test
{
    int value;
public:
    Test() { cout << "T1" << endl;   }
    Test(int n ) { cout << value << endl; }
};

int main()
{
    Test a[2];
    Test b(5);
    Test *c = new Test[3];
    delete [] c;
}
```

Problem #1.7: Please fill in the blanks for the following program to make the program output the followings:
(1,3) r = 5
(1,3) r = 5

```cpp
#include <iostream>
using namespace std;

class Point
{
public:
    int x,y;
    Point(int px,int py): x(px), y(py) { }
};

class Circle
{
public:
    int radius;
    Point b;
    Circle (int px,int py,int r): _____ { }

    Circle (Circle &o): _____ { }
};

int main()
{
    Circle c1(1,3,5);

    Circle c2 = c1;

    cout << "(" << c1.b.x << "," << c1.b.y << ")" << " r = " << c1.radius << endl;

    cout << "(" << c2.b.x << "," << c2.b.y << ")" << " r = " << c2.radius << endl;
}
```

Problem #1.8: What is the output of the following program?

```
#include <iostream>
using namespace std;

class Double
{
public:
    double value;
    Double() { };
    Double(double n):value(n) { };
    Double(const Double & db) { value = db.value + 1; }
};

Double Output(Double *db)
{
    cout << db->value;
    db->value = db->value * 3;
    return *db;
}

int main()
{
    Double a(1);
    Double b = a;
    Double c = Output( &b );

    cout << c.value;

    Double d;
    d = a;

    cout << d.value;
}
```

Problem #1.9:
A student wrote the following program and expected to see outputs as
0
5
Unfortunately, the outputs of this program are actually:
1
1
Could you please help fix this program?

```cpp
#include <iostream>
using namespace std;

class Double
{
public:
    double value;
    Double(double n = 1 )    { value = n; }
    Double GetMyself()       { return *this; }
};

int main()
{
    Double db;

    cout << db.value << endl;

    db.GetMyself() = 5;

    cout << db.value << endl;
}
```

Problem #1.10: The following program will crash when it is run. Please fix it.

```cpp
#define _CRT_SECURE_NO_WARNINGS // To suppress Visual C++ error messages
                                // on the use of strcpy()
#include <iostream>
#include <cstring>
using namespace std;

class student
{
public:
    student(const char *name, const double &score) {
        this->name = new char[strlen(name)+1];
        strcpy(this->name, name);
        this->score = score;
    }
    void output() {
        cout << "Student's name is: " << name << endl;
        cout << "Score is : " << score << endl;
    }
    ~student() {    delete [] name;        }
private:
    char *name;
    double score;
};

int main()
{
    student A("ABC",100);

    student B = A;              // Does this use copy constructor or assignment operator?

    B.output();

    student *C = &A;

    C->output();
}
```

11

Problem #1.11: The following program will crash when it is run. Please fix it.

```cpp
#define _CRT_SECURE_NO_WARNINGS // To suppress Visual C++ error messages
                                // on the use of strcpy()

#include <iostream>
#include <cstring>
using namespace std;

class student
{
public:
    student(const char *name, const double &score) {
        this->name = new char[strlen(name)+1];
        strcpy(this->name, name);
        this->score = score;
    }
    student(const student &st) {
        this->name = new char[strlen(st.name)+1];
        strcpy(this->name,st.name);
        this->score = st.score;
    }
    void output() {
        cout << "Student's name is: " << name << endl;
        cout << "Score is : " << score << endl;
    }
    ~student() {    delete [] name;     }
private:
    char *name;
    double score;
};

int main()
{
    student A("ABC",100);
    student B = A;
    B.output();
    student *C = &A;
    C->output();
    B = A;              // Does this use copy constructor or assignment operator?
    B.output();
}
```

12

```cpp
#include <iostream>
using namespace std;
// You cannot use strcpy(), strcat() or strcmp() functions.

class mystring
{
public:
    mystring() {   str=new char[1];   str[0] = '\0';   length = 0;   }
    mystring (const char *source);
    mystring (const mystring& s);
    mystring& operator= (const mystring& s);
    ~mystring();
    int size() const;              // return length back;
    char* c_str();                 // return c-string back
private:
    char *str;
    int length;
};

int main()
{
    int i;
    mystring *s[2];                // What does this mean? Please explain it.
    for(i=0;i<2;i++)
        s[i] = new mystring();     // What does this mean? Please explain it.
    *s[0] = "Review";              // What does this mean? Please explain it.
    *s[1] = "Session";

    cout << s[0]->c_str() << " " << s[1]->c_str() << endl;

    *s[0] = "For";
    *s[1] = "CS32";
    cout << s[0]->c_str() << " " << s[1]->c_str() << endl;

    for(i=0;i<2;i++)
        delete s[i];               // What does this mean? Please explain it.
}
```

Problem #1.12(a): Please write an implementation for the destructor:

13

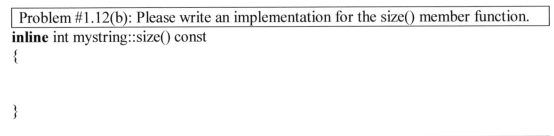

Problem #1.12(b): Please write an implementation for the size() member function.

inline int mystring::size() const
{

}

Problem #1.12(c): Please write an implementation for the c_str() member function. Please make use of the inline keyword.

Problem #1.12(d): Please write an implementation for the constructor: mystring(const char *source). Please note that you cannot use strlen() and strcpy() to aid your implementation.

Problem #1.12(e): Please write an implementation for the copy constructor: mystring(const mystring& s). Please note that you cannot use strlen() and strcpy() to aid your implementation.

Problem #1.12(f): Please write an implementation for the assignment operator:
Please note that you cannot use strlen() and strcpy() to aid your implementation.

Practice 1 – Solution

1.1: Compilation error because of missing `public` keyword in class A. It should be:
```
class A
{
public:
    string str;
};
```
1.2: 14222999

1.3: CS32

1.4: **<u>Note:</u>** If you do not declare any constructor / destructor, then the C++ compiler will make default constructor(s) / destructor for you. If you declare a constructor / destructor, then C++ compiler will not make a default one for you.

The student class needs a user-defined default constructor so that this statement
```
student s;
```
can then work. Or we can just initialize student objects with some values like:
```
student s("", 0);
```
The fixed program is as the following:
```cpp
#include <iostream>
#include <string>
using namespace std;
class student
{
public:
    student() {
        this->name = "";
        this->score = 0;
    }
    student(const string &name, const double &score) {
        this->name = name;
        this->score = score;
    }
    void output() {
        cout << "Student's name is: " << name << endl;
        cout << "Score is : " << score << endl;
    }
private:
    string name;
    double score;
};
int main()
{
    student s;
    // Or just initialize student objects with some values like:
    // student s("", 0);
    s.output();
}
```

1.5: Using `delete p;` is wrong. It should be `delete [] p;`
When we use `new` without using [], then the delete statement does not need [].
When we use `new` by using [], then the delete statements needs to use [].

1.6: Change `Test(int n): { cout << value << endl; }`
to `Test(int n): value(n) { cout << value << endl; }`

16

1.7: The Circle class should be defined as:

```cpp
class Circle
{
public:
    int radius;
    Point b;
    Circle(int px, int py, int r) : b(px, py), radius(r) {}

    Circle(Circle &o) : b(o.b), radius(o.radius) {}
};
```

1.8: 271

1.9:

Change   `Double(double n = 1) { value = n; }`

to   `Double(double n = 0) { value = n; }`

and change   `Double GetMyself() { return *this; }`

to   `Double& GetMyself() { return *this; }`

1.10: The original program does not have a copy constructor, so both objects A and B have their private data member `name` point to the same address. Thus, when the destructors got called, it would try to delete a storage that's already been deleted, hence causing the program to crash. A copy constructor is needed:

```cpp
student(const student& st) {
    this->name = new char[strlen(st.name) + 1];
    strcpy(this->name, st.name);
    this->score = st.score;
}
```

1.11: The original program does not have an assignment operator, so both objects A and B have their private data member `name` point to the same address. Thus, when the destructors got called, it would try to delete a storage that's already been deleted, hence causing the program to crash. An assignment operator is needed:

```cpp
student &operator=(const student &st) {
    if (&st == this) // if assigning to itself, return itself.
        return *this;
    delete[] this->name;
    this->name = new char[strlen(st.name) + 1];
    strcpy(this->name, st.name);
    this->score = score;
}
```

1.12: mystring *s[2]; means that s is an array that can store 2 pointers pointing to mystring objects. So we need to point each mystring pointer to a mystring object by going through each element i to do this: s[i] = new mystring(); Thus, s[0] is the address of the mystring object, and *s[0] is that mystring object. *s[0] = "Review" will utilize the assignment operator. Finally, in order to delete the storage, we need to do "delete s[i]" instead of "delete *s[i]" because we should delete the memory space beginning at that address.

1.12(a): The destructor can be implemented as:

```cpp
mystring::~mystring()
{
    delete[] str;
}
```

17

1.12(b): The size member function can be implemented as:
```cpp
inline int mystring::size() const
{
    return length;
}
```

1.12(c): The c_str member function can be implemented as:
```cpp
inline char* mystring::c_str()
{
    return str;
}
```

1.12(d): The constructor can be implemented as:
```cpp
mystring::mystring(const char *source)
{
    int len = 0;
    const char *ptr = source;

    while (*ptr++) len++;

    length = len;

    str = new char[len + 1];
    char *dest = str;

    while (*dest++ = *source++);
}
```

1.12(e): The copy constructor can be implemented as:
```cpp
mystring::mystring(const mystring& s)
{
    str = new char[s.length + 1];
    char *source = s.str;
    char *dest = str;
    while (*dest++ = *source++);
    length = s.length;
}
```

1.12(f): The assignment operator can be implemented as:
```cpp
mystring& mystring::operator=(const mystring& s)
{
    if (&s == this)
        return *this;

    delete[] str;
    str = new char[s.length + 1];

    char *source = s.str;
    char *dest = str;

    while (*dest++ = *source++);

    length = s.length;
}
```

Practice 2 – Linked List, Stack, and Queue

> Problem #2.1: Below is a program to construct polynomials and display the constructed polynomials on the screen. However, there are some bugs in the program that make it CRASH almost every time it is executed. Please help fix it.

```
#include <iostream>
using namespace std;

struct Node {
    Node(int c, int e): coef(c), exp(e), next(nullptr) {}
    int coef, exp;
    Node *next;
};

class poly {
public:
    poly() : head(nullptr) { }
    ~poly();
    void addNewTerm(int c, int e);
    void display();
private:
    Node *head;
};

poly::~poly() {
    Node *ptr = head;
    while (ptr->next != nullptr) {        // !?
        ptr = ptr->next;                  // !?
        Node *temp = ptr;                 // !?
        delete temp;
    }
    head = nullptr;
}

void poly::addNewTerm(int c, int e) {
    Node *current = new Node(c, e);
    if (head == nullptr)
        head = current;
    else {
        Node *ptr = head;
        while (ptr != nullptr)            // !?
            ptr = ptr->next;
        ptr->next = current;
    }
}
```

19

```cpp
void poly::display() {

    if (head == nullptr) {
        cout << "No polynomial terms were entered!!" << endl;
        return;
    }

    cout << head->coef << "*X^" << head->exp;

    Node *ptr = head->next;

    while (ptr->next != nullptr) {                // !?
        if (ptr->coef > 0)
            cout << " +";

        cout << ptr->coef << "*X^" << ptr->exp;

        ptr = ptr->next;
    }
    cout << endl;
}

int main() {
    int choice, c, e;
    poly p;

    do {
        cout << "Please select an option:" << endl;
        cout << "1) Add a new polynomial term." << endl;
        cout << "2) Display current polynomials." << endl;
        cout << "3) Quit." << endl;

        cin >> choice;

        switch (choice) {
            case 1:
                cout << "Please enter a coefficient followed by an exponent:";
                cin >> c >> e; // 3 2 means 3x^2
                p.addNewTerm(c, e);
                break;
            case 2:
                p.display();
                break;
        }
    } while (choice != 3);
}
```

Problem #2.2: Below is a program to construct a Singly Linked List. Please answer the question in the next page.

```cpp
#include <iostream>
#include <cassert>
using namespace std;

class LinkedList
{
public:
    LinkedList(): head(nullptr) { }
    ~LinkedList()
    {
        Node *temp;
        while (head != nullptr)
        {
            temp = head;
            head = head->next;
            delete temp;
        }
    }
    void append(int value) // Append to the end of the linked list
    {
        Node *current = new Node(value, nullptr);
        if (head == nullptr)
            head = current;
        else
        {
            Node *ptr = head;
            while (ptr->next != nullptr)
                ptr = ptr->next;
            ptr->next = current;
        }
    }
    int JosephusCircle(int N);
private:
    struct Node
    {
        int num;
        Node *next;
        Node(int n, Node* ptr): num(n), next(ptr) {}
    };
    Node *head;
};
```

Problem #2.2 (Continued): You and your friends got caught by 100 cannibals in some weird rainforest. Unfortunately, there is no way you can call 911. Fortunately, you overheard these cannibals talking in English about the game they will play on you guys. It's called Josephus Circle that they will make you guys stand in a circle, announce the number N, and every Nth person in the circle will be eaten. Only the last person standing will be freed. Although you are skeptical about whether they are actually cannibals, you decide to write a program to figure out where you should stand in the circle to be the last person standing. Unfortunately, when you open your laptop, you only have a singly linked list C++ program there and a fragmented JosephusCircle() member function. Hurry up!! Your life is on the line…..

Example: Suppose there are 5 people there in a circle numbered from 1 to 5.
1st round: Number 2 is eaten.
2nd round: Number 4 is eaten.
3rd round: Number 1 is eaten.
4th round: Number 5 is eaten.
Number 3 is the last guy standing…

```cpp
int main()
{
    int i, N;
    for(N=1;N<=7;N++)
    {
        LinkedList circle;

        for(i=1;i<=N;i++)     // Append Number 1 through N to the Linked List
            circle.append(i);

        cout << "Number " << circle.JosephusCircle(2); // Every 2nd person is @!#%^

        cout << " is the last guy standing." << endl;
    }
}
```

// The outputs for the above program are:

Number 1 is the last guy standing.
Number 1 is the last guy standing.
Number 3 is the last guy standing.
Number 1 is the last guy standing.
Number 3 is the last guy standing.
Number 5 is the last guy standing.
Number 7 is the last guy standing.

```cpp
int LinkedList::JosephusCircle(int N)
{
    Node* ptr = head;
    Node* prev = nullptr;
    int count;
    while(head->next != nullptr)
    {
        for( count=1; count<N; count++)
        {

            _____


            _____

            if(ptr == nullptr)

                _____


        }

        Node *temp = ptr;

        if(head == ptr)

            _____

        else

            _____

        ptr = ptr->next;

        if(ptr == nullptr)

            _____


        delete temp;         // see you on the other side …
    }

    return head->num;
}
```

Problem #2.3: Please fill in the missing C++ codes to use Singly Linked List to
support all the functionalities in this specific Stack class.

```cpp
#include <iostream>
using namespace std;
class Stack    {
public:
     Stack()    {    head = nullptr; }
     Stack(const Stack &s);
     ~Stack();
     void push(int n);
     void pop();
     int top() const;
     bool empty() const;
     Stack& operator=(const Stack& s);
private:
     struct Node {
          Node *next;
          int value;
          Node(int v, Node* n) : value(v), next(n) { }  // There is no default constructor!
     };
     Node *head;
};
int main()
{
     Stack A;
     for(int i=0;i<5;i++)
          A.push(i);
     Stack B(A);              // This uses the copy constructor
     Stack C;
     C = A;                   // This uses the assignment operator
     while( !C.empty() ) {
          cout << C.top() << endl;
          C.pop();
     }
}
Stack::~Stack()
{
     while(head != nullptr) {     // Please add codes below




     }
}
```

```
void Stack::push(int n)
{    // Please add codes below



}

int Stack::top() const
{
     if( empty() ) {
          cout << "Stack is empty!!" << endl;
          exit(1);
     }
     // Please add code(s) below



}

bool Stack::empty() const
{    // Please add code(s) below



}

void Stack::pop()
{
     if( empty() ) {
          cout << "Stack is empty!!" << endl;
          return ;
     }
     // Please add code(s) below



}
```

```cpp
Stack::Stack(const Stack &s)
{
    if(s.head == nullptr)
    {
        head = nullptr;
        return ;
    }
    head = new Node(s.head->value, nullptr);

    // Please add codes below




}

Stack& Stack::operator=(const Stack& s)
{
    if(&s != this)
    {   // Please add codes below




    }
    return *this;
}
```

Problem #2.4: The following program uses Doubly Linked List with head and tail pointers to implement the Queue. Please fill in the blanks to complete this program.

```cpp
#include <iostream>
using namespace std;

class Queue {
public:
    Queue() { head = tail = nullptr; }
    Queue(const Queue &s);
    ~Queue();
    void push(int n);
    void pop();
    int front() const;
    bool empty() const;
    Queue& operator=(const Queue& s);
private:
    struct Node {
        Node *prev, *next;
        int value;
        Node(int v, Node *prv, Node* nxt) : value(v), prev(prv), next(nxt) { }
    };
    Node *head, *tail;
};

int main()
{
    Queue A;
    for (int i = 0; i<5; i++)
        A.push(i);
    Queue B(A);
    Queue C;
    C = B;
    while (!C.empty()) {
        cout << C.front() << endl;
        C.pop();
    }
}

Queue::~Queue()
{
    while ( _____ ) {
        Node *temp = head;
        head = head->next;
        delete temp;
    }
}
```

27

```cpp
void Queue::push(int n)
{
    if ( _____ )
        head = tail = new Node(n, nullptr, nullptr);
    else {
        tail->next = new Node(n, tail, nullptr);

        tail = _____
    }
}

int Queue::front() const
{
    if (empty()) {
        cout << "Queue is empty!!" << endl;
        exit(1);
    }
    return _____
}

bool Queue::empty() const
{
    if (head == _____ )
        return true;
    return false;
}

void Queue::pop()
{
    if (empty()) {
        cout << "Queue is empty!!" << endl;
        return;
    }
    Node *temp = head;
    head = head->next;
    if (head != nullptr)
        head->prev = nullptr;

    delete _____
}
```

```cpp
Queue::Queue(const Queue &s)
{
    if (s.empty())
    {
        head = nullptr;
        return;
    }
    tail = head = new Node( _____ );

    for (Node* source = s.head->next, *dest = head; source != nullptr;
        source = source->next, dest = dest->next)
    {
        dest->next = new Node(source->value, dest, nullptr);

        tail = _____
    }
}

Queue& Queue::operator=(const Queue& s)
{
    if (&s != this)
    {
        if (s.head == nullptr)
        {
            head = nullptr;
            return *this;
        }
        tail = head = new Node( _____ );

        for (Node* source = s.head->next, *dest = head; source != nullptr;
            source = source->next, dest = dest->next)
        {
            dest->next = new Node(source->value, dest, nullptr);

            tail = _____
        }
    }
    return *this;
}
```

Problem #2.5: A student wrote the following program to determine whether an input string is a palindrome or not by using a stack. A palindrome is a sequence of characters that reads the same backward or forward. For example, ABBA is a palindrome and ABCA is not a palindrome. Unfortunately, there are 3 lines of codes that are missing. Could you please help this student fill in the blanks?

```cpp
#include <iostream>
#include <string>
#include <stack>
using namespace std;

int main()
{
    string str;
    cout << "Please enter a string: ";
    cin >> str;
    int i, len = str.size();

    stack<char> s;          // Instead of implementing stack by ourselves, C++ has
                            // standard template libraries (STL) for Stack.

    for( i = 0 ; i < len / 2 ; i++ )
        s.push( str[i] );

    if _____

        _____


    for ( ; i < len ; i++ )
    {
        if (s.top() != str[i])
            break;

        _____
    }

    if(i == len)
        cout << str << " is a palindrome." << endl;
    else
        cout << str << " is NOT a palindrome." << endl;
}
```

Problem #2.6: Please use a stack to reverse elements in a queue. The correct outputs from the following program should be:
9876543210

```cpp
#include <iostream>
#include <queue>
#include <stack>
using namespace std;

int main()
{
    int i;
    queue<int> q;      // Instead of implementing stack by ourselves, C++ has
                       // standard template libraries (STL) for Queue and Stack.
    stack<int> s;
    for(i=0;i<10;i++)
        q.push(i);

    while(!q.empty())
    {


    }
    while(!s.empty())
    {



    }
    while(!q.empty())
    {
        cout << q.front();
        q.pop();
    }
    cout << endl;
}
```

31

Problem #2.7: Please fill in the blanks to simulate a queue by using 2 stacks.

```cpp
#include <iostream>
#include <queue>
#include <stack>
#include <cassert>
using namespace std;
class twoStacks
{
public:
    twoStacks() { }
    void push(int value) {
        s1.push(value);
    }
    void moveFromS1toS2() {
        // Only move elements from Stack 1 to Stack 2 when Stack 2 is empty
        // because the order of elements in Stack 2 should be ordered like a Queue.
        if (s2.empty()) {
            if (s1.empty()) {
                cerr << "twoStacks are empty!" << endl;
                exit(1);
            }

            while ( _____ ) {

                s2.push( _____ );


                _____

            }
        }
    }
    int front() const {


        _____

        return s2.top();
    }
    void pop() {


        _____

        s2.pop();
    }
private:
    stack<int> s1;        // push elements into s1
    stack<int> s2;        // pop elemtns from s2
};
```

32

```cpp
int main()
{
    int i;
    queue<int> q;
    twoStacks ts;
    for(i=0;i<10;i++) {         // push numbers 0~9 to the queue
        q.push(i);
        ts.push(i);
    }

    q.pop();                    // pop 0 out of the queue
    ts.pop();

    for(i=10;i<20;i++) {        // push numbers 10~19 to the queue
        q.push(i);
        ts.push(i);
    }

    while( !q.empty() )   {
        assert( q.front() == ts.front() );
        q.pop();
        ts.pop();
    }
}
```

Problem #2.8: Please fill in the blanks to simulate a stack by using 2 queues.

```cpp
#include <iostream>
#include <queue>
#include <stack>
#include <cassert>
using namespace std;
class twoQueues {
public:
    twoQueues() { }
    void push(int value);
    int pop();
private:
    queue<int> q1;
    queue<int> q2;
};

int main() {
    int i;
    stack<int> s;
    twoQueues tq;

    for(i=0;i<10;i++)   {
        s.push(i);
        tq.push(i);
    }
    for(i=0;i<10;i++)   {
        assert( s.top() == tq.pop() );
        s.pop();
    }
}

void twoQueues::push(int value)   {
    // push into q1 if both are empty.
    if (q1.empty() && q2.empty())
        q1.push(value);
    // push into q2 if q1 is empty
    else if (q1.empty() && !q2.empty())
        q2.push(value);
    // push into q1 if q2 is empty
    else if (!q1.empty() && q2.empty())
        q1.push(value);
    else {
        cerr << "Error: Both queues have values!" << endl;
        exit(1);
    }
}
```

// The idea is to pop the last element in q1 or q2 depending on whether
// q1 or q2 is empty. This is how to simulate a stack with 2 queues.

```
int twoQueues::pop() {
    if( q1.empty() && q2.empty() ) {
        cerr << "Error: Both queues are empty!" << endl;
        exit(1);
    }
    else if( q1.empty() && !q2.empty() ) {
        int temp;
        while ( _____ ) {

            temp = _____
            q2.pop();

            if ( _____ )
                return temp;

            q1.push( _____ );
        }
    }
    else if( !q1.empty() && q2.empty() ) {
        int temp;
        while ( _____ )
        {
            temp = _____
            q1.pop();

            if ( _____ )
                return temp;

            q2.push( _____ );
        }
    }
    else {
        cerr << "Error: Both queues have values!" << endl;
        exit(1);
    }
}
```

Problem #2.9: Please use the following algorithm to convert the infix string, (A+B)*C−D, to postfix string by filling in the blanks in the table.

initialize the postfix string to empty
initialize the operator stack to empty
for each character chr in the infix string
    switch (chr)
        case '(':
            push chr onto the top of the operator stack
            break
        case ')':
            while the character at the top of the operator stack is not '('
                append the character at the top of the operator stack to postfix string
                pop the operator stack to remove the character at the top
            pop the operator stack to remove the character at the top (to remove '(')
            break
        case '+':
        case '-':
        case '*':
        case '/':
            while the operator stack is not empty and
                the character at the top of the operator stack is not '(' and
                the precedence of operator stack top >= the precedence of chr
                append the character at top of the operator stack to the postfix string
                pop the operator stack to remove the character at the top
            push chr onto the top of the operator stack
            break
        default:
            append chr to the end of the postfix string
            break
while the operator stack is not empty
    append the character at top of the operator stack to the postfix string
    pop the operator stack to remove the character at the top

Operand	Operator Stack	Postfix String
(		
A		A
+	(+	A
B		AB
)		
*		
C		
−		AB+C*
D		
		AB+C*D−

Practice 2 – Solution

2.1: The destructor should be:

```
poly::~poly() {
    Node *ptr = head;
    while (ptr != nullptr) {
        Node *temp = ptr;
        ptr = ptr->next;
        delete temp;
    }
    head = nullptr;
}
```

The addNewTerm() member function should be:

```
void poly::addNewTerm(int c, int e) {
    Node *current = new Node(c, e);
    if (head == nullptr)
        head = current;
    else {
        Node *ptr = head;
        while (ptr->next != nullptr)
            ptr = ptr->next;
        ptr->next = current;
    }
}
```

The display() member function needs to change the while loop from:

```
while (ptr->next != nullptr)
```

to:

```
while (ptr != nullptr)
```

2.2: The JosephusCircle member function can be implemented as:

```
int LinkedList::JosephusCircle(int N)
{
    Node* ptr = head;
    Node* prev = nullptr;
    int count;
    while (head->next != nullptr)
    {
        for (count = 1; count<N; count++)
        {
            prev = ptr;
            ptr = ptr->next;
            if (ptr == nullptr)
                ptr = head;
        }
        Node *temp = ptr;
        if (head == ptr)
            head = ptr->next;
        else
            prev->next = ptr->next;
        ptr = ptr->next;

        if (ptr == nullptr)
            ptr = head;

        delete temp;       // see you on the other side …
    }
    return head->num;
}
```

2.3:   Member functions can be implemented as the followings:

```cpp
Stack::~Stack()
{
    while (head != nullptr) {
        Node *temp = head;
        head = head->next;
        delete temp;
    }
}
void Stack::push(int n)
{
    head = new Node(n, head);
}

int Stack::top() const
{
    if (empty()) {
        cout << "Stack is empty!!" << endl;
        exit(1);
    }
    return head->value;
}

bool Stack::empty() const
{
    if (head == nullptr)
        return true;
    return false;
}
void Stack::pop()
{
    if (empty()) {
        cout << "Stack is empty!!" << endl;
        return;
    }
    Node *temp = head;
    head = head->next;
    delete temp;
}
Stack::Stack(const Stack &s)
{
    if (s.head == nullptr) {
        head = nullptr;
        return;
    }
    head = new Node(s.head->value, nullptr);

    for (Node* source = s.head->next, *dest = head;
        source != nullptr;
        source = source->next, dest = dest->next) {
        dest->next = new Node(source->value, nullptr);
    }
}
```

```cpp
Stack& Stack::operator=(const Stack& s)
{
    if (&s != this) {
        if (s.head == nullptr) {
            head = nullptr;
            return *this;
        }
        head = new Node(s.head->value, nullptr);

        for (Node* source = s.head->next, *dest = head;
            source != nullptr;
            source = source->next, dest = dest->next) {
            dest->next = new Node(source->value, nullptr);
        }
    }
    return *this;
}
```

2.4: Member functions can be implemented as the followings:

```cpp
Queue::~Queue() {
    while (head != nullptr) {
        Node *temp = head;
        head = head->next;
        delete temp;
    }
}
void Queue::push(int n) {
    if (head == nullptr)
        head = tail = new Node(n, nullptr, nullptr);
    else {
        tail->next = new Node(n, tail, nullptr);
        tail = tail->next;
    }
}
int Queue::front() const {
    if (empty()) {
        cout << "Queue is empty!!" << endl;
        exit(1);
    }
    return head->value;
}
bool Queue::empty() const {
    if (head == nullptr)
        return true;
    return false;
}
void Queue::pop() {
    if (empty()) {
        cout << "Queue is empty!!" << endl;
        return;
    }
    Node *temp = head;
    head = head->next;
    if (head != nullptr)
        head->prev = nullptr;
    delete temp;
}
```

```cpp
Queue::Queue(const Queue &s)
{
    if (s.empty())
    {
        head = nullptr;
        return;
    }
    tail = head = new Node(s.head->value, nullptr, nullptr);

    for (Node* source = s.head->next, *dest = head; source != nullptr;
        source = source->next, dest = dest->next) {
        dest->next = new Node(source->value, dest, nullptr);
        tail = dest->next;
    }
}
Queue& Queue::operator=(const Queue& s)
{
    if (&s != this)
    {
        if (s.head == nullptr)
        {
            head = nullptr;
            return *this;
        }
        tail = head = new Node(s.head->value, nullptr, nullptr);

        for (Node* source = s.head->next, *dest = head;
            source != nullptr;
            source = source->next, dest = dest->next)
        {
            dest->next = new Node(source->value, dest, nullptr);
            tail = dest->next;
        }
    }
    return *this;
}
```

2.5:   The main function can be implemented as:

```cpp
int main() {
    string str;
    cout << "Please enter a string: ";
    cin >> str;
    int i, len = str.size();
    stack<char> s;
    for (i = 0; i < len / 2; i++)
        s.push(str[i]);
    if (len % 2)
        i++;
    for (; i < len; i++)
    {
        if (s.top() != str[i])
            break;
        s.pop();
    }
    if (i == len)
        cout << str << " is a palindrome." << endl;
    else
        cout << str << " is NOT a palindrome." << endl;
}
```

40

2.6:   The two while loops should be:

```
while (!q.empty())
{
      s.push(q.front());
      q.pop();
}
while (!s.empty())
{
      q.push(s.top());
      s.pop();
}
```

2.7:   The 3 member functions should be like the followings:

```
void moveFromS1toS2() {
     if (s2.empty()) {
          if (s1.empty()) {
               cerr << "twoStacks are empty!" << endl;
               exit(1);
          }
          while (!s1.empty()) {
               s2.push(s1.top());
               s1.pop();
          }
     }
}
int front() {
     moveFromS1toS2();
     return s2.top();
}
void pop() {
     moveFromS1toS2();
     s2.pop();
}
```

2.8:   The missing codes should be like:

```
     else if (q1.empty() && !q2.empty()) {
          int temp;
          while (!q2.empty()) {
               temp = q2.front();
               q2.pop();
               if (q2.empty())
                    return temp;
               q1.push(temp);
          }
     }
     else if (!q1.empty() && q2.empty()) {
          int temp;
          while (!q1.empty())
          {
               temp = q1.front();
               q1.pop();
               if (q1.empty())
                    return temp;
               q2.push(temp);
          }
     }
```

2.9: The table should be filled in as:

Operand	Operator Stack	Postfix String
(	(	
A	(	A
+	(+	A
B	(+	AB
)		AB+
*	*	AB+
C	*	AB+C
−	−	AB+C*
D	−	AB+C*D
		AB+C*D−

Practice 3 – Inheritance and Polymorphism

Problem #3.1: If the following program doesn't compile, why not? If it does compile, what is the output when it is run?

```
#include <iostream>
using namespace std;

virtual void hello()
{
    cout << "Hello World!" << endl;
}

int main()
{
    hello();
}
```

Problem #3.2: What is the output of the following program? How many times will class A's destructor get called?

```
#include <iostream>
using namespace std;

class A
{
public:
    ~A()
    {
        cout << "A is destructed!" << endl;
    }
};

int main()
{
    A a;
    a.~A();    // !!!
}
```

Problem #3.3: What is the output of the following program?

```cpp
#include <iostream>
using namespace std;

class Base
{
public:
    Base() { cout << "1" ; }
    ~Base() { cout << "3"; }
};

class Derived : public Base
{
public:
    Derived() { cout << "2"; }
    ~Derived() { cout << "4"; }
};

int main()
{
    Derived d;   // How about Base b; ?
}
```

Problem #3.4: What is the output of the following program? Do you see any issues with the following program?

```cpp
#include <iostream>
using namespace std;
class Base
{
public:
    Base() { cout << "1" ; }
    ~Base() { cout << "3"; }
};

class Derived : public Base
{
public:
    Derived() { cout << "2"; }
    ~Derived() { cout << "4"; }
};

int main()
{
    Base *base_ptr = new Base();
    Derived *derived_ptr = new Derived();
}
```

```cpp
#include <iostream>
using namespace std;

class A
{
public:
    virtual void output(int n)
    {
        cout << "A" << n << endl;
    }
};

class B : public A
{
public:
    virtual void output(int n)
    {
        cout << "B" << n << endl;
    }
};

int main()
{
    B b;
    b.output(5);
}
```

Problem #3.6: In Problem 3.5, without changing the main() function, please fill in the blanks inside B's member function, output(int n), to generate the following output?
A1000
B5

```cpp
class B : public A
{
public:
    virtual void output(int n)
    {
        A::_____

        cout << "B" << n << endl;
    }
};
```

Problem #3.7: What is the output of the following program?

```cpp
#include <iostream>
using namespace std;

class Base
{
public:
    void output(int n)
    {
        cout << "Hello Base" << n << endl;
    }
};

class Derived : public Base
{
public:
    void output()          // This hides the output(int n) member function from Base class
    {
        cout << "Hello Derived Class!" << endl;
    }
};

int main()
{
    Base b;
    b.output(1);
    Derived d;
    d.output();
    d.Base::output(2);
}
```

```cpp
#include <iostream>
using namespace std;

class Base
{
public:
    Base() { }
    ~Base( ) {}
    virtual void creation()
    {
        cout << "Base::creation()" << endl;
    }
    virtual void cleanup( )
    {
        cout << "Base::cleanup()" << endl;
    }
};

class Derived : public Base
{
public:
    Derived ( )    {   creation( ) ;   }
    ~Derived ( )   {   cleanup( );     }
};

class Last : public Derived
{
public :
    Last( ) { }
    ~Last() {   cleanup( );   }
    void cleanup()
    {
        cout << "Last::cleanup()" << endl;
    }
};

int main()
{
    Last L;
}
```

Problem #3.9: What is the output of the following program?

```cpp
#include <iostream>
using namespace std;

class A
{
public:
    void output()              {    cout << "A" << endl;    }
};

class B : public A
{
public:
    void output()              {    cout << "B" << endl;    }
};

int main()
{
    A *a = new A();            a->output();
    A *b = new B();            b->output();
    delete a, b;
}
```

Problem #3.10: What is the output of the following program?

```cpp
#include <iostream>
using namespace std;

class A
{
public:
    void output()              {    cout << "A" << endl;    }
};

class B : public A
{
public:
    virtual void output()      {    cout << "B" << endl;    }
};

int main()
{
    A *a = new A();            a->output();
    A *b = new B();            b->output();
    delete a, b;
}
```

```cpp
#include <iostream>
using namespace std;

class A
{
public:
    virtual void output()      {    cout << "A" << endl;    }
};

class B : public A
{
public:
    void output()              {    cout << "B" << endl;    }
};

int main()
{
    A *a = new A();            a->output();
    A *b = new B();            b->output();
    delete a, b;
}
```

```cpp
#include <iostream>
using namespace std;

class A
{
public:
    virtual void output()      {    cout << "A" << endl;    }
};

class B : public A
{
public:
    virtual void output()      {    cout << "B" << endl;    }
};

int main()
{
    A *a = new A();            a->output();
    A *b = new B();            b->output();
    delete a, b;
}
```

```
#include <iostream>
using namespace std;

class Base
{
public:
    Base() { cout << "1" << endl; }
    ~Base() { cout << "4" << endl; }
};
class Derived : public Base
{
public:
    Derived() { cout << "2" << endl; }
    ~Derived() { cout << "3" << endl; }
};
int main()
{
    Base *ptr = new Derived();
    delete ptr;
}
```

```
#include <iostream>
using namespace std;

class Base
{
public:
    Base() { cout << "1" << endl; }
    ~Base() { cout << "4" << endl; }
};
class Derived : public Base
{
public:
    Derived() { cout << "2" << endl; }
    ~Derived() { cout << "3" << endl; }
};
int main()
{
    Derived d;
    Base *b = &d;
    Base *ptr = new Derived();
    delete ptr;
}
```

Problem #3.15: If we add the **virtual** keyword to the **destructors** in both the Base class and the Derived class in Problem #3.13 and #3.14, then what is the output of the modified programs? Why do we need virtual destructors?

Problem #3.16: Which line(s) below can cause compilation error(s)?

```
#include <iostream>
using namespace std;

class Base { };
class D1 : public Base { };
class D2 : public Base { };

int main()
{
    Base *ptr1 = new D1();      // Line 1

    Base *ptr2 = new D2();      // Line 2

    D1 *ptr3 = new Base();      // Line 3

    D1 *ptr4 = new D2();        // Line 4

    delete ptr1;                // Line 5

    delete ptr2;                // Line 6
}
```

Problem #3.17: If the following program doesn't compile, why not? If it does compile, what is the output when it is run?

```
#include <iostream>
using namespace std;

class Base
{
public:
    virtual void output() = 0;  // This makes Base class an Abstract Base Class (ABC)
};
class Derived : public Base
{
public:
    void output() { cout << "Hello World!" << endl; }
};

int main()
{
    Base b;
    b.output();
    Derived d;
    d.output();
}
```

52

```cpp
#include <iostream>
using namespace std;

class Base
{
public :
    virtual ~Base()
    {
        cout << "1" << endl;
    }
};

class D1: public Base
{
public:
    virtual ~D1()
    {
        cout << "2" << endl;
    }
};

class D2: public D1
{
public:
    virtual ~D2()
    {
        cout << "3" << endl;
    }
};

int main()
{
    Base * ptr = new D2;

    delete ptr;
}
```

Problem #3.19: What is the output of the following program?

```cpp
#include <iostream>
using namespace std;

class Person
{
public:
    void Play()
    {   cout << "Person::Play" << endl;             };
    void Study()
    {   cout << "Person::Study" << endl;            }
};

class Student: public Person
{
public:
    virtual void Study()
    {   cout << "Student::Study" << endl;           }
};

class CS_Student : public Student
{
public:
    void Play()
    {   cout << "CS_Student::Play!" <<endl;         }
    void Study()
    {   cout << "CS_Student::Study!" << endl; }
};

void activity( Person &s )
{
    s.Play();
    s.Study();
}

int main()
{
    CS_Student cs_student;

    activity(cs_student);
}
```

Problem #3.20: What is the output of the following program?

```cpp
#include <iostream>
using namespace std;

class Person
{
public:
    void Play()
    {    cout << "Person::Play" << endl;              };
    void Study()
    {    cout << "Person::Study" << endl;             }
};

class Student: public Person
{
public:
    virtual void Study()
    {    cout << "Student::Study" << endl;            }
};

class CS_Student : public Student
{
public:
    void Play()
    {    cout << "CS_Student::Play!" <<endl;          }
    void Study()
    {    cout << "CS_Student::Study!" << endl;        }
};

void activity( Student &s )
{
    s.Play();
    s.Study();
}

int main()
{
    CS_Student cs_student;
    activity(cs_student);
}
```

55

Problem #3.21: What is the output of the following program?

```cpp
#include <iostream>
using namespace std;

class Person
{
public:
    void Play()
    {    cout << "Person::Play" << endl;              };
    void Study()
    {    cout << "Person::Study" << endl;             }
};

class Student: public Person
{
public:
    void Play()
    {    cout << "Student::Play" << endl;             }
    virtual void Study()
    {    cout << "Student::Study" << endl;            }
};

class CS_Student : public Student
{
public:
    void Play()
    {    cout << "CS_Student::Play!" <<endl;   }
    void Study()
    {    cout << "CS_Student::Study!" << endl;        }
};

void activity( Student &s )
{
    s.Play();
    s.Study();
}

int main()
{
    CS_Student cs_student;
    activity(cs_student);
}
```

Problem #3.22: What is the output of the following program?

```cpp
#include <iostream>
using namespace std;

class Person
{
public:
    virtual void Play()
    {   cout << "Person::Play" << endl;          };
    virtual void Study()
    {   cout << "Person::Study" << endl;         }
};

class Student: public Person
{
public:
    virtual void Play()
    {   cout << "Student::Play" << endl;         }
    void Study()
    {   cout << "Student::Study" << endl;        }
};

class CS_Student : public Student
{
public:
    virtual void Play()
    {   cout << "CS_Student::Play!" <<endl;   }
    void Study()
    {   cout << "CS_Student::Study!" << endl;    }
};

void activity( Person &s )
{
    s.Play();
    s.Study();
}

int main()
{
    CS_Student cs_student;

    activity(cs_student);
}
```

Problem #3.23: What is the output of the following program?

```cpp
#include <iostream>
using namespace std;

class Other
{
public:
    Other(int n) { cout << "Other::" << n + 10 << endl; }
    ~Other() { cout << "~Other::-15" << endl; }
};

class Base
{
    int value;
public:
    Base(int n): value(n) { cout << "Base::" << n << endl; }
    ~Base() { cout << "~Base::" << -value << endl; }
};

class D1 : public Base
{
    Other o;
public:
    D1(int n):Base(n),o(n) { cout << "D1::" << n + 5 << endl; }
    ~D1() { cout << "~D1::-10" << endl; }
};

int main()
{
    D1 d(5);
}
```

58

Problem #3.24: Please complete the implementation of the Base class so that the output of this program is:
CS32

```cpp
#include <iostream>
using namespace std;
class Base
{




};

class Derived : public Base
{
public:
    ~Derived()
    {
        cout << "CS";
    }
};

int main()
{
    Base* ptr = new Derived;
    delete ptr;
    cout << endl;
}
```

Problem #3.25: A student wrote the following program and expected the output as:
Base value is: 0
Derived value is: 10
However, there is a compilation error in this program. Please help fix it.

```cpp
#include <iostream >
using namespace std;

class Base
{
private:
    int base_value;
public:
    Base(int n): base_value(n) {}
    int getValue() { return base_value; }
};

class Derived : public Base
{
private:
    int derived_value;
public:
    Derived(int n): Base(n) { derived_value = n + 10; }
    int getValue() { return derived_value; }
    void output()
    {
        cout << "Base value is: " << Base::base_value << endl;
        cout << "Derived value is: " << getValue() << endl;
    }
};

int main()
{
    Derived d(0);
    d.output();
}
```

Practice 3 – Solution

3.1: Compilation error because only member functions can be virtual.

3.2: 2 times.

3.3: 1243

Note: Base b; gives the outputs: 13

3.4: 112

Note: This program allocates 2 objects by using the new statement, but does not de-allocate (delete) the objects. So the destructor never gets called, hence causing memory leak.

3.5: B5

3.6: Class B should be defined as:

```
class B : public A
{
public:
    virtual void output(int n)
    {
        A::output(1000);
        cout << "B" << n << endl;
    }
};
```

3.7: Hello Base1
Hello Derived Class!
Hello Base2

3.8: Base::creation()
Last::cleanup()
Base::cleanup()

3.9: A
A

3.10: A
A

3.11: A
B

3.12: A
B

3.13: 1
2
4

3.14: 1
2
1
2
4
3
4

61

3.15: For 3.13, the outputs become:

1
2
3
4

For 3.14, the outputs become:

1
2
1
2
3
4
3
4

Virtual destructors are needed to properly free the storage of the derived classes. Without virtul destructors, the destructor in the Base class will always get called instead of calling the destructor in the Derived class first and then calling the destructor in the Base class second.

3.16: **Line 3** causes a compilation error because a derived class pointer cannot point to the base class unless through forced conversion by the user by using dynamic_cast. Also, **Line 4** causes a compilation error too because the sibling class pointer cannot point to the other sibling class (in which both inherit from the same parent class) unless through forced conversion by the user by using dynamic_cast.

3.17: Since the Base class has declared a pure virtual member function, output(), the Base class becomes an Abstract Base Class that cannot be instantiated.

3.18: 3
2
1

3.19: Person::Play
Person::Study

3.20: Person::Play
CS_Student::Study!

3.21: Student::Play
CS_Student::Study!

3.22: CS_Student::Play!
CS_Student::Study!

3.23: Base::5
Other::15
D1::10
~D1::-10
~Other::-15
~Base::-5

3.24: The Base class should be:
```
class Base
{
public:
    virtual ~Base()
    {
        cout << "32";
    }
};
```
3.25: Change this line:
```
cout << "Base value is: " << Base::base_value << endl;
```
to:
```
cout << "Base value is: " << Base::getValue() << endl;
```

Practice Midterm 1

Problem #	Maximal Possible Points	Received
1.1	3	
1.2	5	
1.3	5	
1.4	5	
1.5	5	
2	3	
3.1	4	
3.2	5	
Total	35	

```cpp
#include <iostream>
#include <cassert>
using namespace std;

class LinkedList
{
public:
    LinkedList(): head(nullptr) { }
    ~LinkedList();
    void addToList(int value);        // Append to the end of the linked list
    void reverse();                   // Reverse the linked list
    void output();
    bool findNthFromLast(int N, int &value);
private:
    struct Node
    {
        int num;
        Node *next;
    };
    Node *head;
};

void LinkedList::output()
{
    Node *ptr = head;
    cout << "The elements in the list are: ";
    while(ptr!=nullptr)
    {
        cout << ptr->num << " ";
        ptr = ptr->next;
    }
    cout << endl;
}

int main()
{
    LinkedList list;
    for(int i=1;i<=10;i++)
        list.addToList(i);

    list.output();
    list.reverse();
    list.output();
}
```

Problem #1.1: Please complete the implementation of the **destructor**.

Problem #1.2: Please write an implementation of the addToList member function.

Problem #1.3: Please complete the implementation of the reverse member function.

```cpp
void LinkedList::reverse()
{
    Node *nextNode = nullptr,*prevNode = nullptr, *current = head;
    while(current != nullptr)
    {    // Hint: Only 4 lines of codes are needed inside the while loop



    }
    head = prevNode;
}
```

Problem #1.4: Suppose we add a new member function called findNthFromLast()
to find the N-th node from the end of the list, where N being 1 means the last node,
N being 2 the second-to-last, etc.   Use the reverse member function to complete
the implementation of findNthFromLast() member function. If the list has at least N
nodes, then assign to the variable value the number that is stored in that node and
return true; otherwise, leave the variable value unchanged and return false.   Don't
forget to call the reverse function to restore the linked list to its original state.

```cpp
bool LinkedList::findNthFromLast(int N, int &value)
{
    if (N <= 0)
        return false;



}
```

Problem #1.5: There is a more efficient way to solve problem #1.4 without using reverse() function. The idea is to scan first to count the total number of nodes in the linked list. Once we know how many nodes are in the linked list, the second time we scan the list, the Nth node from the end of list can be easily calculated. Please use this idea to implement this member function findNthFromLast().

```cpp
bool LinkedList::findNthFromLast(int N, int &value)
{




















}
// Your implementation should pass the following test program
int main()
{
    int value = 999;
    LinkedList list;

    for(int i=1;i<=10;i++)
        list.addToList(i);

    assert( ! list.findNthFromLast(0, value) && value == 999);
    assert( ! list.findNthFromLast(11,value) && value == 999);
    assert( list.findNthFromLast(1,value) && value == 10);
    assert( list.findNthFromLast(2,value) && value == 9);
    assert( list.findNthFromLast(10,value) && value == 1);

}
```

Problem #2: Please fill in the blanks below to make the program generate the following outputs:
1+2i
6+7i
6+7i
6+7i

```cpp
#include <iostream>
using namespace std;

class Complex
{
private:
    double r,i;
public:
    Complex(): _____ {}

    Complex(int c_r,int c_i): _____ {}

    void output()
    {
        cout << r << "+" << i << "i" << endl;
    }
};

int main()
{
    Complex a,b;

    a = Complex(1, 2);
    a.output();

    b = Complex(6, 7);
    b.output();

    a = b;

    a.output();
    b.output();
}
```

Problem #3: The implementation below will CRASH because it's missing a copy constructor and an assignment operator.

```cpp
#include <iostream>
using namespace std;

class Triangle
{
public:
    Triangle() {    p = new Point[3];    }

    // Triangle(Triangle &t);
    // Triangle& Triangle::operator=(const Triangle &t);

    Triangle(int x1, int y1, int x2, int y2, int x3, int y3)
    {
        p = new Point[3];
        p[0].x = x1; p[0].y = y1;
        p[1].x = x2; p[1].y = y2;
        p[2].x = x3; p[2].y = y3;
    }
    Triangle::~Triangle() {         delete[] p;      }
private:
    struct Point
    {
        int x, y;
        Point(int px = 0, int py = 0) : x(px), y(py) { }
    };
    Point *p;
};

int main()
{
    Triangle *array[3];
    array[0] = new Triangle(1, 1, 1, 3, 3, 1);
    array[1] = new Triangle(2, 2, 2, 6, 6, 2);
    array[2] = new Triangle(3, 3, 3, 9, 9, 3);

    Triangle c2 = *array[0];

    c2 = *array[1];

    for (int i = 0; i<3; i++)
        delete array[i];
}
```

Problem #3.1: Please write an implementation of the copy constructor.

```cpp
Triangle::Triangle(Triangle &t)
{



}
```

Problem #3.2: Please write an implementation of the assignment operator.

```cpp
Triangle& Triangle::operator=(const Triangle &t)
{



}
```

Practice Midterm 1 – Solution

1.1: The destructor can be implemented as:

```
LinkedList::~LinkedList()
{
    Node *temp;
    while (head != nullptr)
    {
        temp = head;
        head = head->next;
        delete temp;
    }
}
```

1.2: The addToList member function can be implemented as:

```
void LinkedList::addToList(int value)
{
    Node *current = new Node;
    current->num = value;
    current->next = nullptr;
    if (head == nullptr)
        head = current;
    else
    {
        Node *ptr = head;
        while (ptr->next != nullptr)
            ptr = ptr->next;
        ptr->next = current;
    }
}
```

1.3: The reverse member function can be implemented as

```
void LinkedList::reverse()
{
    Node *nextNode = nullptr, *prevNode = nullptr, *current = head;
    while (current != nullptr) {
        nextNode = current->next;
        current->next = prevNode;
        prevNode = current;
        current = nextNode;
    }
    head = prevNode;
}
```

1.4: The findNthFromLast member function can be implemented as:

```cpp
bool LinkedList::findNthFromLast(int N, int &value)
{
    if (N <= 0)
        return false;
    reverse();
    Node *ptr = head;
    int n = 0;
    while (ptr != nullptr) {
        n++;
        if (n == N) {
            value = ptr->num;
            reverse();
            return true;
        }
        ptr = ptr->next;
    }
    reverse();
    return false;
}
```

1.5: The findNthFromLast member function can be implemented as:

```cpp
bool LinkedList::findNthFromLast(int N, int &value)
{
    if (N <= 0)
        return false;
    Node *ptr = head;
    int i, M = 0;
    // M is the number of nodes in the linked list.
    while (ptr != nullptr)
    {
        M++;
        ptr = ptr->next;
    }
    if (N > M)
        return false;
    for (i = 1, ptr = head; i < (M - N + 1); i++)
        ptr = ptr->next;
    value = ptr->num;

    return true;
}
```

2: The Complex class can be implemented as:

```cpp
class Complex
{
private:
    double r, i;
public:
    // Please complete the missing codes below.
    Complex() : r(0), i(0) {}
    Complex(int c_r, int c_i) : r(c_r), i(c_i) {}
    void output()
    {
        cout << r << "+" << i << "i" << endl;
    }
};
```

3.1:   The copy constructor can be implemented as:

```
Triangle::Triangle(Triangle &t)
{
    p = new Point[3];
    for (int i = 0; i<3; i++)
        p[i] = t.p[i];
}
```

3.2:   The assignment operator can be implemented as:

```
Triangle& Triangle::operator=(const Triangle &t)
{
    if (&t == this)
        return *this;
    delete[] p;
    p = new Point[3];
    for (int i = 0; i<3; i++)
        p[i] = t.p[i];
    return *this;
}
```

Practice 4 – Recursion

Problem #4.1: What is the output of the program below?

```
#include <iostream >
using namespace std;

void foo()
{
    int i,j;
    for(i=0;i<4;i++)
        for(j=0;j<4;j++)
            cout << i << j << endl;
}

int main()
{
    foo();
}
```

Problem #4.2: Please implement a recursive function foo2() to generate the same outputs in problem #4.1.

```
#include <iostream >
using namespace std;

void foo2(int a[],int count)
{
    if(count == 2)
    {



    }
    for(int i=0;i<4;i++)
    {



    }
}

int main()
{
    int a[3];
    foo2(a,0);
}
```

75

Problem #4.3: Please implement the reverse() function to recursively reverse a
C-String. Both reverse2() and reverse() functions should produce the same outputs.

```cpp
#include <iostream>
#include <string>
#include <cassert>
using namespace std;
void reverse2(string &str, int len)
{
    int i;
    char temp;
    for (i = 0; i<len / 2; i++)
    {
        temp = str[i];
        str[i] = str[len - i - 1];
        str[len - i - 1] = temp;
    }
}
void reverse(string &str, int start, int end)
{
    char temp;
    if (start < end)
    {    // In each reverse() function call, we should swap 2 characters in the string



    }
}
int main()
{
    string str1 = "ABCDE", str2 = "ABCDE";

    reverse(str1, 0, str1.size());
    reverse2(str2, str2.size());

    assert(str1 == str2);
}
```

Problem #4.4: Please implement the reversePrint() function to recursively print the string backward. Both reversePrint2() and reversePrint() functions should produce the same outputs: *7654321*

```cpp
#include <iostream >
#include <string>
using namespace std;

void reversePrint2(string &str)
{
    for(int i=str.size()-1; i>=0; i--)
        cout << str[i];
}

void reversePrint(string &str, int counter)
{




}

int main()
{
    string str = "1234567";

    reversePrint(str,0);        cout << endl;

    reversePrint2(str);         cout << endl;
}
```

Problem #4.5: Please implement the isPalindrome() function to recursively print the string backward. Both isPalindrome2() and isPalindrome() functions should produce the same outputs. For example, given the inputs:
open
kayak
aabbaa
The program should produce the following outputs:
open is not a Palindrome.
kayak is a Palindrome.
aabbaa is a Palindrome.

```
#include <iostream >
#include <string>
using namespace std;

bool isPalindrome2(string &str)
{
    for(int i=0;i<str.size()/2;i++)
        if(str[i] != str[ str.size() - i - 1] )
            return false;
    return true;
}

bool isPalindrome(string &str, int start, int end)
{




}

int main()
{
    string str;
    cin >> str;
    if( isPalindrome(str, 0, str.size()) && isPalindrome2(str) )
        cout << str << " is a Palindrome." << endl;
    else
        cout << str << " is not a Palindrome." << endl;
}
```

Problem #4.6: Please implement the fib() function to recursively calculate the Fibonacci number. A Fibonacci number is defined as a sequence of numbers that every number is the sum of the previous two numbers except for the first two numbers being 1. Thus, Fibonacci numbers are: 1   1   2   3   5   8   13 … etc. Both fib2() and fib() functions should produce the same outputs.

```cpp
#include <iostream>
#include <cassert>
using namespace std;

int fib2(int n)
{
     int *arr = new int[n+1];
     int value;
     arr[0] = 1;
     arr[1] = 1;
     for(int i=2;i<=n;i++)
          arr[i] = arr[i-1] + arr[i-2];
     value = arr[n];
     delete [] arr;
     return value;
}

int fib(int n)
{



}

int main()
{
     for(int i = 1 ; i < 5 ; i++ )
          assert( fib(i) == fib2(i) );
}
```

Problem #4.7: Please implement the isPrimeNumber() function to recursively test whether a given number is a prime number. Both isPrimeNumber() and isPrimeNumber2() functions should produce the same outputs.
For example, given the inputs:
8
13
5557
The program should produce the following outputs:
8 is not a prime number.
13 is a prime number.
5557 is a prime number.

```cpp
#include <iostream >
using namespace std;

bool isPrimeNumber2(int number)
{
    for(int i=2; i*i < number ; i++)
        if( number % i == 0)
                return false;
    return true;
}

bool isPrimeNumber(int number, int i=2)
{



}

int main()
{
    int value;
    cin >> value;
    if ( isPrimeNumber(value) && isPrimeNumber2(value) )
        cout << value << " is a prime number." << endl;
    else
        cout << value << " is not a prime number." << endl;
}
```

Practice 4 – Solution

4.1: 00
01
02
03
10
11
12
13
20
21
22
23
30
31
32
33

4.2: foo2 function can be implemented as:

```cpp
void foo2(int a[], int count)
{
    if (count == 2)
    {
        for (int j = 0; j<count; j++)
            cout << a[j];
        cout << endl;
        return;
    }
    for (int i = 0; i<4; i++)
    {
        a[count] = i;
        foo2(a, count + 1);
    }
}
```

4.3: reverse2 function can be implemented as:

```cpp
void reverse(string &str, int start, int end)
{
    char temp;
    if (start < end)
    {
        // either
        temp = str[start];
        str[start] = str[end - 1];
        str[end - 1] = temp;
        reverse(str, start + 1, end - 1);
        // or
        // reverse(str,start+1,end-1);
        // temp = str[start];
        // str[start] = str[end-1];
        // str[end-1] = temp;
        // Both work….
    }
}
```

4.4:   The reversePrint function can be implemented as:

```
void reversePrint(string &str, int counter)
{
    if (counter == str.size())
        return;
    // either
    reversePrint(str, counter + 1);
    cout << str[counter];
    // or
    // cout << str[ str.size() - counter - 1];
    // reversePrint(str,counter + 1);
}
```

4.5:   The isPalindrome function can be implemented as:

```
bool isPalindrome(string &str, int start, int end)
{
    if (start >= end)
        return true;
    return (str[start] == str[end - 1] &&
            isPalindrome(str, start + 1, end - 1));
}
```

4.6:   The fib function can be implemented as:

```
int fib(int n)
{
    if (n == 0 || n == 1)
        return 1;
    return fib(n - 1) + fib(n - 2);
}
```

4.7:   The isPrimeNumber function can be implemented as:

```
bool isPrimeNumber(int number, int i = 2)
{
    if (i*i > number)
        return true;
    if (number % i == 0) // Divisible by i => Not a prime number
        return false;
    return isPrimeNumber(number, i + 1);
}
```

Practice 5 – Templates, Iterators, STL

Problem #5.1: What is the output of the following program?

```cpp
#include <iostream>
using namespace std;

template <typename T>
T max( T a,T b)
{
    cout << "Use T max()" <<endl;
    if( a > b)
        return a;
    return b;
}

double max(double a,double b)
{
    cout << "Use double max()" << endl;
    if( a > b)
        return a;
    return b;
}

int main()
{
    double a = 5, b = 3;
    cout << max( 1.20, 3.40) << endl;
    cout << max( a, b) << endl;
}
```

Problem #5.2: What is the output of the following program?

```cpp
#include <iostream>
using namespace std;

int sum(int* begin, int* end)
{
    cout << "Use int sum()" << endl;
    int total = *begin++;
    while(begin != end)
    {
        total += *begin;
        begin++;
    }
    return total;
}

template <typename T>
T sum(T* begin, T* end)
{
    cout << "Use T sum()" << endl;
    T total = *begin++;
    while (begin != end)
    {
        total += *begin;
        begin++;
    }
    return total;
}

int main()
{
    double arr[] = { 0.5 , 1.5 , 2.5 , 3.5 };
    int values[] = { 1 , 2 , 3 , 4 };
    cout << "Sum of arr[] is " << sum(&arr[0],&arr[4]) << endl;
    cout << "Sum of values[] is " << sum(values , values + 4) << endl;
}
```

Problem #5.3: Please write the implementation of min() and max() functions so that the outputs from the following program are:
min of arr[] is : 1.5
min of values[] is : -1
max of arr[] is : 5.5
max of values[] is : 5
min of the first 2 elements in arr : 4.5

```cpp
#include <iostream>
using namespace std;
template<typename T>
T min(T* begin, T* end)
{
    T min_value = *begin++;




    return min_value;
}
// Write your max() function implementation below...




int main()
{
    double arr[] = {   5.5, 4.5, 3.5, 2.5, 1.5 };
    int values[] = {   1, 2, 3, 4, -1, 5 };
    cout << "min of arr[] is : " << min(arr, arr + 5) << endl;
    cout << "min of values[] is : " << min(values, values + 6) << endl;
    cout << "max of arr[] is : " << max(arr, arr + 5) << endl;
    cout << "max of values[] is : " << max(values, values + 6) << endl;
    cout << "min of the first 2 elements in arr : " << min(arr, arr + 2) << endl;
}
```

Problem #5.4: Please fill in the blanks for the min_max() function below so that the outputs from the following program are:
min of arr[] is : 1.5, max of arr[] is : 5.5
min of values[] is : -1, max of values[] is : 5

```cpp
#include <iostream>
using namespace std;

template<typename T>
struct pairs { T min_value, max_value; };

template<typename T>
_____    min_max(T* begin, T* end)
{
    pairs<T> p;
    p.min_value = p.max_value = *begin++;
    while(begin != end)
    {
        if(*begin > p.max_value)


        _____

        if(*begin < p.min_value)


        _____



        _____

    }
    return p;
}
int main()
{
    double arr[] = {   5.5, 4.5, 3.5, 2.5, 1.5 };
    int values[] = {   1, 2, 3, 4, -1, 5 };

    pairs<double> dp;
    pairs<int> ip;

    dp = min_max(arr, arr + 5);
    ip = min_max(values, values + 6);

    cout << "min of arr[] is : " << dp.min_value
        << ", max of arr[] is : " << dp.max_value << endl;

    cout << "min of values[] is : " << ip.min_value
        << ", max of values[] is : " << ip.max_value << endl;
}
```

86

Problem #5.5: Please fill in the blanks for the min_max() function below so that the outputs from the following program are:
1 2 3 4 5 6 7 8 9 10

```cpp
#include <iostream>
#include <algorithm>
using namespace std;

class myClass
{
public:
    myClass() { }

    void setValue(const int& v) { value = v; }

    int getValue() _____ { return value; }

private:
    int value;
};

bool operator<(const myClass &a, const myClass &b) {
    return a.getValue() < b.getValue();
}

int main()
{
    myClass mc[20];

    for(int i=0;i<10;i++)
        mc[i].setValue( 10 - i );

    cout << "Before Sorting:" << endl;

    for(int i=0;i<10;i++)
        cout << mc[i].getValue() << endl;

    sort(mc, _____ );

    cout << "After Sorting:" << endl;

    for(int i=0;i<10;i++)
        cout << mc[i].getValue() << endl;
}
```

Problem #5.6: Please convert the program in Problem #5.5 by filling in the blanks below to use template so that the outputs from the following program are:
1 2 3 4 5 6 7 8 9 10

```cpp
#include <iostream>
#include <string>
#include <algorithm>
using namespace std;


_____

class myClass
{
public:
    myClass() { }
    void setValue(const T& v) { value = v; }
    T getValue() const { return value; }

private:

    _____

};


_____

bool operator<(_____ &a, _____ &b) {
    return a.getValue() < b.getValue();
}

int main()
{
    myClass<int> mc[10];

    for (int i = 0; i<10; i++)
        mc[i].setValue(10 - i);

    sort(mc, mc + 10);

    for (int i = 0; i<10; i++)
        cout << mc[i].getValue() << " ";
    cout << endl;
}
```

88

Problem #5.7: Please fill in the blanks below to allow myclass to store string data so that the outputs from the following program are:
ABC Hello XYZ

```cpp
#include <iostream>
#include <string>
#include <algorithm>
using namespace std;

template<typename T>
class myClass
{
public:
    myClass() { }

    T getValue() const { return value; }

    bool operator<(_____ &b)
    {
        return value < _____ ;
    }

    myClass& operator=(const string &str)
    {
        _____
        return *this;
    }
private:
    T value;
};

int main()
{
    myClass<string> mc[3];

    mc[0] = "Hello";
    mc[1] = "ABC";
    mc[2] = "XYZ";

    sort(mc, mc + 3);

    for (int i = 0; i<3; i++)
        cout << mc[i].getValue() << " ";
    cout << endl;
}
```

Problem #5.8: What is the output of the following circular Queue program? Please make sure you trace through the code by hands.

```cpp
#include <iostream>
using namespace std;

class myQueue
{
public:
    myQueue(int cap = 5) : capacity(cap), head(-1), tail(-1)
    {
        if (cap <= 0)
        {
            cout << "Error: Capacity <= 0!" << endl;
            exit(1);
        }
        arr = new int[capacity];
    }
    ~myQueue()
    {
        delete [] arr;
    }
    inline bool isFull() const
    {
        return ((tail + 1) % capacity == head);
    }
    inline bool empty() const
    {
        return (head == -1);
    }
    void push(const int& value);
    void pop();
    int front() const;
private:
    int *arr;
    int head, tail;
    int capacity;
};
int myQueue::front() const
{
    if (empty())
    {
        cout << "Error: Front() failed because Queue is empty!!" << endl;
        exit(1);
    }
    return arr[head];
}
```

```cpp
void myQueue::push(const int& value)
{
    if (isFull())
    {
        cout << "Error: Push() failed because Queue is Full!" << endl;
        return;
    }
    tail = (tail + 1) % capacity;
    arr[tail] = value;
    if (head == -1)
        head = tail;
}

void myQueue::pop()
{
    if (empty())
    {
        cout << "Error: Pop() failed because Queue is empty!!" << endl;
        return;
    }
    if (head == tail)
        head = tail = -1;
    else
        head = (head + 1) % capacity;
}

int main()
{
    myQueue mq;

    for (int i = 0; i<6; i++)
        mq.push( i );

    for (int i = 0; i<5; i++)
    {
        cout << mq.front() << endl;
        mq.pop();
    }
}
```

Problem #5.9: Please fill in the blanks below to allow the program in Problem #5.8 to use different data types. For example, the program below should output the followings:
Error: Push() failed because Queue is Full!
0.5
1.5
2.5
3.5
4.5

```cpp
#include <iostream>
using namespace std;

template<typename T>
class myQueue
{
public:
    myQueue(int cap = 5) : capacity(cap), head(-1), tail(-1)
    {
        if (cap <= 0)
        {
            cout << "Error: Capacity <= 0!" << endl;
            exit(1);
        }
        arr = new _____
    }
    ~myQueue()
    {
        delete [] arr;
    }
    inline bool isFull() const
    {
        return ((tail + 1) % capacity == head);
    }
    inline bool empty() const
    {
        return (head == -1);
    }
    void push(const _____ &value);
    void pop();
    _____ front() const;
private:
    _____ *arr;
    int head, tail;
    int capacity;
};
```

```cpp
template<typename T>
_____     myQueue _____ ::front() const
{
    if (empty())
    {
        cout << "Error: Front() failed because Queue is empty!!" << endl;
        exit(1);
    }
    return arr[head];
}
template<typename T>
void myQueue _____ ::push(const _____ & value)
{
    if (isFull())
    {
        cout << "Error: Push() failed because Queue is Full!" << endl;
        return;
    }
    tail = (tail + 1) % capacity;
    arr[tail] = value;
    if (head == -1)
        head = tail;
}
template<typename T>
void myQueue _____ ::pop()
{
    if (empty())
    {
        cout << "Error: Pop() failed because Queue is empty!!" << endl;
        return;
    }
    if (head == tail)
        head = tail = -1;
    else
        head = (head + 1) % capacity;
}
int main()
{
    myQueue<double> mq;
    for (int i = 0; i<6; i++)
        mq.push( i + 0.5);
    for (int i = 0; i<5; i++) {
        cout << mq.front() << endl;
        mq.pop();
    }
}
```

93

Problem #5.10: Below is an implementation of myVector to simulate the vector implementation in C++ STL. The idea of a re-sizeable array is that every time the vector runs out of space, it re-allocates 2 times as large as the original array and moves everything from the original array to this newly allocated array. Please fill in the blanks in push_back() member functions so that the outputs from this program are:
0 1 2 3 4

```cpp
#include <iostream>
using namespace std;

template<typename T>
class myVector
{
public:
    myVector()
    {
        capacity = 1;
        length = 0;
        arr = new T[capacity];
    }
    ~myVector()
    {
        if(arr != nullptr)
            delete [] arr;
    }
    T at(int idx)
    {
        return arr[idx];
    }
    void push_back(const T& value);
    void clear()
    {
        if(arr != nullptr)
            delete [] arr;
        arr = nullptr;
    }
private:
    T *arr;
    int length;
    int capacity;
};
```

```cpp
void myVector<T>::push_back(const T& value)
{
    if(length == capacity)
    {
        capacity *= 2;

        T *new_storage = _____

        for(int i=0;i<length;i++)
            new_storage[i] = arr[i];

        T *temp = arr;

        arr = _____

        delete [] temp;
    }


    _____

}

int main()
{
    myVector<int> mv;

    for(int i=0;i<5;i++)
        mv.push_back( i );

    for(int i=0;i<5;i++)
        cout << mv.at(i) << " ";
    cout << endl;
}
```

Problem #5.11: The following program will crash when it is run. Please help fix it.

```cpp
#include <iostream>
#include <vector>
using namespace std;

int main()
{
    vector<int> vec;

    for(int i=0;i<5;i++)
        vec.push_back(i);

    vector<int>::iterator it = vec.begin();

    while(it <= vec.end())          // Hmmm....?
    {
        cout << *it << endl;
        it++;
    }
}
```

Problem #5.12: The following program will crash when it is run. Please help fix it.

```cpp
#include <iostream>
#include <list>
using namespace std;

int main()
{
    list<double> l;

    for (int i = 0; i<5; i++)
        l.push_back(i + 0.5);

    for( list<double>::iterator it = l.begin(); it != l.end(); it++ )
    {
        cout << *it << endl;
        it++;
    }
}
```

Problem #5.13: Please fill in the blanks below so that the outputs from this program are:
0 1 2
3 4 5 6 7 8 9 10 11 12

```cpp
#include <iostream>
#include <vector>
#include <list>
using namespace std;

int main()
{
    vector< list<int> > vec;
    list<int> list01,list02;

    for(int i=0;i<3;i++)
        list01.push_back(i);

    for(int i=0;i<10;i++)
        list02.push_back(i + 3);

    vec.push_back(list01);
    vec.push_back(list02);

    _____  vec_it = vec.begin();

    while(vec_it != vec.end() )
    {
        _____  list_it = vec_it->begin();

        while( list_it != vec_it->end() )
        {
            cout << *list_it << " ";

            _____
        }

        _____

        cout << endl;
    }
}
```

Problem #5.14: A fellow student is helping United Nations Mine Action Service (UNMAS) to record the positions of identified landmines in a historic battle field in a database. Unfortunately, the data he received is string data that require him to find the (x,y) coordinates manually. He decided to write a program to automate this process. Below is a small test program he wrote for a small dataset. Unfortunately, he drank too much coffee that he accidentally erased some codes. Please fill in the blanks below to help this student so that the outputs from this program are:
The bombs are located at:
(0 , 3)
(1 , 2)
(2 , 7)
(3 , 0)

```cpp
#include <iostream>
#include <vector>
#include <string>
#include <map>
using namespace std;
void findBombs( string field[],    map<int, vector<int> > &mp)
{
    for (int i = 0; i<5; i++)
    {
        vector<int> row;
        for (int j = 0; j < field[i].size(); j++)
        {
            if (field[i][j] == 'B')
                row.push_back(j);
        }
        mp[i] = _____
    }
}
void output( map<int, vector<int> > &mp)
{
    cout << "The bombs are located at:" << endl;
    map<int, vector<int> >::iterator    map_it = _____
    while ( map_it != mp.end() )
    {
        vector<int>::iterator            vec_it = _____
        // or vector<int>::iterator     vec_it = (*map_it).second.begin();
        while ( vec_it != map_it->second.end() )
        {
            cout << "( " << map_it->first << " , " << _____ << " ) " << endl;
            vec_it++;
        }
        _____
    }
}
```

98

```cpp
int main()
{
    string field[5] =
    {   "...B....",
        "..B.....",
        ".......B",
        "B.......",
        "........"
    };

    map<int, vector<int> > mp;

    findBombs( field, mp );

    output( mp );
}
```

Problem #5.15: What is the output of the following program? Will the destructor of myClass be called? If not, why?

```cpp
#include <iostream>
#include <vector>
using namespace std;

class myClass
{
public:
    myClass(int v): value(v)
    {
        cout << v << endl;
    }
    ~myClass()
    {
        cout << -value << endl;
    }
private:
    int value;
};

int main()
{
    vector<myClass*> vec;

    vec.push_back( new myClass(4) );
    vec.push_back( new myClass(8) );
}
```

Problem #5.16: Please fill in the blanks below so that the outputs are:
Apple,Banana,Blackberry,Pineapple,Strawberry

```cpp
#include <iostream>
#include <vector>
#include <string>
#include <algorithm>
using namespace std;

template <typename T>
class MyClass
{
public:
    MyClass(T * begin , int n )
    {
        T *end = begin+n;

        while( _____ )
        {

            name.push_back( _____ );
            begin++;
        }
        sort(_____ , _____ );
    }
    void output()
    {
        _____ it = name.begin();
        cout << *it++;
        for( ; it != name.end() ; it++ )
            cout << "," << *it;
        cout << endl;
    }

private:
    vector<T> name;
};

int main()
{
    string str[5] = { "Pineapple","Strawberry","Banana","Apple","Blackberry"};

    MyClass<string> mc(str,5);

    mc.output();
}
```

Practice 5 – Solution

5.1: Use double max()
3.4
Use double max()
5

5.2: Use T sum()
Sum of arr[] is 8
Use int sum()
Sum of values[] is 10

5.3: The min and max functions can be implemented as:
```
template<typename T>
T min(T* begin, T* end)
{
    T min_value = *begin++;
    while (begin != end) // You can use for-loop too.
    {
        if (*begin < min_value)
            min_value = *begin;
        begin++;
    }
    return min_value;
}
template<typename T>
T max(T* begin, T* end)
{
    T max_value = *begin++;
    while (begin != end)
    {
        if (*begin > max_value)
            max_value = *begin;
        begin++;
    }
    return max_value;
}
```

5.4: The min_max function can be implemented as:
```
template<typename T>
pairs<T> min_max(T* begin, T* end)
{
    pairs<T> p;
    p.min_value = p.max_value = *begin++;
    while (begin != end)
    {
        if (*begin > p.max_value)
            p.max_value = *begin;
        if (*begin < p.min_value)
            p.min_value = *begin;
        begin++;
    }
    return p;
}
```

5.5: The getValue member function should be implemented as:
```
int getValue() const { return value; }
```
The sort function should be used like this:
```
sort(mc, mc + 10);
```

5.6:   The program in Problem 5.5 can be modified as:

```
template<typename T>
class myClass
{
public:
    myClass() { }
    void setValue(const T& v) { value = v; }
    T getValue() const { return value; }
private:
    T value;
};
template<typename T>
bool operator<(const myClass<T> &a, const myClass<T> &b) {
    return a.getValue() < b.getValue();
}
```

5.7:   myClass can be implemented as:

```
template<typename T>
class myClass
{
public:
    myClass() { }
    T getValue() const { return value; }
    bool operator<(const myClass<T> &b)
    {
        return value < b.value; // or b.getValue()
    }
    myClass& operator=(const string &str)
    {
        value = str;
        return *this;
    }
private:
    T value;
};
```

5.8:   Error: Push() failed because Queue is Full!

0

1

2

3

4

5.9:   myQueue can be implemented as:

```cpp
template<typename T>
class myQueue
{
public:
    myQueue(int cap = 5) : capacity(cap), head(-1), tail(-1)
    {
        if (cap <= 0)
        {
            cout << "Error: Capacity <= 0!" << endl;
            exit(1);
        }
        arr = new T[capacity];
    }
    ~myQueue()
    {
        delete [] arr;
    }
    inline bool isFull() const
    {
        return ((tail + 1) % capacity == head);
    }
    inline bool empty() const
    {
        return (head == -1);
    }
    void push(const T &value);
    void pop();
    T front() const;
private:
    T *arr;
    int head, tail;
    int capacity;
};
template<typename T>
T myQueue<T>::front() const
{
    if (empty())
    {
        cout << "Error: Front() failed because Queue is empty!!" <<
endl;
        exit(1);
    }
    return arr[head];
}
template<typename T>
void myQueue<T>::push(const T& value)
{
    if (isFull())
    {
        cout << "Error: Push() failed because Queue is Full!" << endl;
        return;
    }
    tail = (tail + 1) % capacity;
    arr[tail] = value;
    if (head == -1)
        head = tail;
}
```

```
template<typename T>
void myQueue<T>::pop()
{
    if (empty())
    {
        cout << "Error: Pop() failed because Queue is empty!!" << endl;
        return;
    }
    if (head == tail)
        head = tail = -1;
    else
        head = (head + 1) % capacity;
}
```

5.10:   The push_back() member function can be implemented as:

```
template<typename T>
void myVector<T>::push_back(const T& value) {
    if (length == capacity) {
        capacity *= 2;
        T *new_storage = new T[capacity];
        for (int i = 0; i<length; i++)
            new_storage[i] = arr[i];
        T *temp = arr;
        arr = new_storage;
        delete[] temp;
    }
    arr[length++] = value;
}
```

5.11:   it <= vec.end() should be it != vec.end() or it < vec.end().

5.12:   Just remove either one of the two   it++

5.13:   The main function can be implemented as:

```
int main()
{
    vector< list<int> > vec;
    list<int> list01, list02;
    for (int i = 0; i<3; i++)
        list01.push_back(i);

    for (int i = 0; i<10; i++)
        list02.push_back(i + 3);

    vec.push_back(list01);
    vec.push_back(list02);

    vector< list<int> >::iterator vec_it = vec.begin();

    while (vec_it != vec.end()) {
        list<int>::iterator list_it = vec_it->begin();

        while (list_it != vec_it->end())
        {
            cout << *list_it << " ";
            list_it++;
        }
        vec_it++;
        cout << endl;
    }
}
```

105

5.14: The functions can be implemented as:

```cpp
void findBombs(string field[], map<int, vector<int> > &mp)
{
    for (int i = 0; i<5; i++)
    {
        vector<int> row;
        for (int j = 0; j< field[i].size(); j++)
        {
            if (field[i][j] == 'B')
                row.push_back(j);
        }
        mp[i] = row;
    }
}
void output(map<int, vector<int> > &mp)
{
    cout << "The bombs are located at:" << endl;
    map<int, vector<int> >::iterator map_it = mp.begin();
    while (map_it != mp.end())
    {
        vector<int>::iterator vec_it = map_it->second.begin();
        // or vector<int>::iterator vec_it = (*map_it).second.begin();
        while (vec_it != map_it->second.end())
        {
            cout<< "( "<<map_it->first<<" , " << *vec_it<<" ) "<<endl;
            vec_it++;
        }
        map_it++;
    }
}
```

5.15: The outputs are:

4

8

The destructor of myClass will never be called because this program never uses `delete` statement to delete any myClass objects. This will cause a memory leak issue. The main function should be implemented as:

```cpp
int main()
{
    vector<myClass*> vec;

    vec.push_back(new myClass(4));
    vec.push_back(new myClass(8));

    delete vec[0];
    delete vec[1];

    vec.pop_back();
    vec.pop_back();
}
```

pop_back() member function only removes the last element which is a pointer to a myClass object, but this never de-allocates the storage for that myClass object, hence never calling the destructor of myClass.

5.16:   MyClass can be implemented as:

```cpp
template <typename T>
class MyClass
{
public:
    MyClass(T * begin, int n)
    {
        T *end = begin + n;
        while (begin != end)
        {
            name.push_back(*begin);
            begin++;
        }
        sort(name.begin(), name.end());
    }
    void output()
    {
        vector<T>::iterator it = name.begin();
        cout << *it++;
        for (; it != name.end(); it++)
            cout << "," << *it;
        cout << endl;
    }
private:
    vector<T> name;
};
```

Practice 6 – Algorithmic Efficiency and Sorting Algorithms

Problem #6.1: What is the Big-O of the function outputQ()?

```cpp
#include <iostream>
using namespace std;

int outputQ(int n)
{
    int counter = 0;
    for(int i=0 ; i < n ; i++ )
    {
        for(int j=0 ; j < n ; j++ )
        {
            counter++;
            break;
        }
    }
    return counter;
}

int main()
{
    cout << outputQ(10) << endl;
}
```

Problem #6.2: What is the Big-O of the function countX()?

```cpp
#include <iostream >
using namespace std;

int countX(int n)
{
    int counter = 0;
    for (int i = 1; i < n; i *= 2)
        for (int j = 1; j <= n; j++)
            for (int k = 1; k <= n; k++)
                counter++;
    return counter;
}

int main()
{
    cout << countX(8) << endl;
}
```

```cpp
#include <iostream >
using namespace std;

int countY(int n)
{
    int counter = 0;
    for(int i=1 ; i < n ; i*= 2 )
        for(int j=1; j < n ; j*= 2 )
            for(int k=1; k < n ; k *= 2)
                counter++;
    return counter;
}

int main()
{
    cout << countY(8) << endl;
}
```

```cpp
#include <iostream >
using namespace std;

int countZ(int n)
{
    int counter = 0;
    int increment = 1, step = 1;
    while( step < n )
    {
        step = step + increment;
        increment++;
        counter++;
    }
    return counter;
}

int main()
{
    cout << countZ(16) << endl;
}
```

```
#include <iostream>
using namespace std;

bool isPrimeNumber(int number)
{
    for(int i=2;i*i < number; i++)
        if( number % i == 0)
                return false;
    return true;
}

int main()
{
    int N;
    cin >> N;
    if(isPrimeNumber(N))    cout << N << " is a prime number." << endl;
    else                    cout << N << " is NOT a prime number." << endl;
}
```

```
#include <iostream >
#include <string>
using namespace std;

bool isPalindrome(string &str)
{
    for(int i=0;i<str.size()/2;i++)
        if(str[i] != str[ str.size() - i - 1] )
                return false;
    return true;
}

int main()
{
    string str;
    cin >> str;
    if( isPalindrome(str))
        cout << str << " is a Palindrome." << endl;
    else
        cout << str << " is not a Palindrome." << endl;
}
```

Problem #6.7: What is the output of the following program?

```cpp
#include <iostream >
#include <algorithm>
using namespace std;

void selectionSort(int A[], int n, int stop)
{
    int start = 0;

    for (int i = 0; i < n; i++)
    {
        int minIndex = i;
        for (int j = i+1; j < n; j++)
        {
            if (A[j] < A[minIndex])
                minIndex = j;
        }
        swap(A[i], A[minIndex]);

        start++;

        if(start == stop)      // This if-statement was added to stop at a specific iteration.
            return ;
    }
}

int main()
{
    int values[12]={ 4, 7, 1, 5, 3, 2, 0, 8, 6, 9, 11, 10};

    selectionSort( values , 12 , 3 );
    // In other words, what is the order of the values after 3 iterations?
    // After 3 iterations, the first 3 numbers in the array should be sorted in ascending
    // order and those 3 values should be the 3 smallest values among these 12 numbers

    for(int i=0;i<12;i++)
        cout << values[i] << " ";
    cout << endl;
}
```

Problem #6.8: What is the output of the following program?

```cpp
#include <iostream >
#include <algorithm>
using namespace std;

void insertionSort(int A[], int n, int stop)
{
     int start = 0;
     for(int s = 2; s <= n; s++)
     {
          int sortMe = A[ s - 1 ];
          int i = s - 2;
          while (i >= 0 && sortMe < A[i])
          {
               A[i+1] = A[i];
               --i;
          }
          A[i+1] = sortMe;
          start++;
          if(start == stop)
               return ;
     }
}

int main()
{
     int values[12]={4,7,1,5,3,2,0,8,6,9,11,10};

     insertionSort(values, 12, 3 );
     // In other words, what is the order of the values after 3 iterations?
     // After 3 iterations, only the first 3 numbers are sorted among the first 3 numbers.
     // The rest of the numbers in the array may have smaller values than any of the first
     // 3 sorted numbers.

     for(int i=0;i<12;i++)
          cout << values[i] << " ";
     cout << endl;
}
```

Problem #6.9: What is the output of the following program?

```cpp
#include <iostream >
#include <algorithm>
using namespace std;

void bubbleSort(int Arr[], int n, int stop)
{
    int start = 0;
    bool atLeastOneSwap;
    do
    {
        atLeastOneSwap = false;

        for (int j = 0; j < (n-1); j++)
        {
            if (Arr[j] > Arr[j + 1])
            {
                swap(Arr[j],Arr[j+1]);
                atLeastOneSwap = true;
            }
        }
        start = start + atLeastOneSwap;
        if(start== stop)
            return ;
    }
    while (atLeastOneSwap == true);
}

int main()
{
    int values[12]={4,7,1,5,3,2,0,8,6,9,11,10};

    bubbleSort(values,12,3);
    // In other words, what is the order of the values after 3 iterations?
    // After 3 iterations, the 3 biggest numbers should be sorted in ascending order and
    // placed at the end of the array. The rest of the numbers in the array will not be
    // bigger than any of the 3 sorted numbers at the end of the array.

    for(int i=0;i<12;i++)
        cout << values[i] << " ";
    cout << endl;
}
```

Problem #6.10: Please fill in the blanks below to complete the implementation of ShellSort.

```cpp
#include <iostream>
#include <algorithm>
using namespace std;

void ShellSort(int Arr[], int n)
{
    bool atLeastOneSwap;

    for(int delta = n/2 ; _____ ; delta /= 2)
    {
        do {
            atLeastOneSwap = _____
            for(int i=0; (i+delta) < n; i++)
            {
                if ( _____ )
                {
                    swap(Arr[i], Arr[ i + delta] );

                    atLeastOneSwap = _____
                }
            }
        }while( atLeastOneSwap );
    }
}

int main()
{
    int values[12]={4,7,1,5,3,2,0,8,6,9,11,10};

    ShellSort(values,12);

    for(int i=0;i<12;i++)
        cout << values[i] << " ";
    cout << endl;
}
```

Problem #6.11: Please fill in the blanks below to complete the implementation of QuickSort.

```cpp
#include <iostream >
#include <algorithm>
using namespace std;

int Partition(int a[], int low, int high)
{
    int pi = low;
    int pivot = a[low];
    do {
        while (low <= high && a[low] <= pivot)


        _____
        while (a[high] > pivot)
            high--;
        if (low < high)
            swap( _____ );
    } while (low < high);

    swap( _____ );
    pi = high;
    return (pi);
}

void QuickSort(int Array[], int First, int Last)
{
    if (Last - First >= 1)
    {
        int PivotIndex;
        PivotIndex = Partition(Array, First, Last);
        QuickSort(Array, First, PivotIndex - 1);        // left
        QuickSort(Array, PivotIndex + 1, Last);         // right
    }
}

int main()
{
    int values[12] = { 4,7,1,5,3,2,0,8,6,9,11,10 };

    QuickSort(values, 0, 11);

    for (int i = 0; i<12; i++)
        cout << values[i] << " ";
    cout << endl;
}
```

Problem #6.12: Please fill in the blanks below to complete the implementation of MergeSort.

```cpp
#include <iostream >
using namespace std;

void merge(int data[], int n1, int n2)
{
    int i = 0, j = 0, k = 0;
    int *temp = new int[n1 + n2];
    int *secondHalf = data + n1;

    while (i < n1 || j < n2)
    {
        if (i == n1)
            temp[k++] = secondHalf[j++];
        else if (j == n2)
            temp[k++] = data[i++];
        else if (data[i] < secondHalf[j])
            temp[k++] = data[i++];
        else
            temp[k++] = secondHalf[j++];
    }
    for (i = 0; i<n1 + n2; i++)
        data[i] = temp[i];
    delete[] temp;
}
void MergeSort(int Arr[], int left, int right)
{
    if (left < right)
    {
        int middle = left + (right - right) / 2;
        MergeSort(Arr, left, middle);
        MergeSort(Arr, middle + 1, right);

        merge(Arr _____, middle - left + 1, right - middle);
    }
}
int main()
{
    int values[12] = { 4,7,1,5,3,2,0,8,6,9,11,10 };
    MergeSort(values, 0, 11);
    for (int i = 0; i<12; i++)
        cout << values[i] << " ";
    cout << endl;
}
```

116

Problem #6.13: Which of the following operations below are **faster** when running them on sorted array of numbers than on unsorted array of numbers?

(1) Find the median
(2) Find the mean.
(3) Find the maximal value in the array.
(4) Find the minimal value in the array.
(5) Calculate the sum of the values.

Problem #6.14: Which of the following sorting algorithms are **stable**?

(1) Quicksort
(2) Insertion Sort
(3) Bubble Sort
(4) Merge Sort

Problem #6.15: Which of the followings are **TRUE**?

(1) In Merge Sort, the merge() operation will visit all the values in the array whenever merge() operation is called.
(2) In Bubble Sort, at current iteration, it will never visit the values that have already been sorted by the previous iterations.
(3) In Selection Sort, at current iteration, it will never visit the values that have already been sorted by the previous iterations.
(4) In Quick Sort, all the values in the array will be visited at every iteration.

Problem #6.16: Which one of the following sorting algorithms always has time complexity of O(n logn) at the worst case scenario?

(1) Merge Sort
(2) Insertion Sort
(3) Bubble Sort
(4) Quick Sort
(5) Shell Sort
(6) Selection Sort

Problem #6.17: Here is a list of 10 numbers that are partially sorted. Which sorting algorithm(s) (quick, merge, bubble, etc.) could have produced the following array after 2 iterations?
Original sequence: 30 50 40 10 20 60 70 90 80 0
Sequence after 2 iterations: 30 10 20 40 50 60 70 0 80 90

(1) Selection Sort
(2) Insertion Sort
(3) Bubble Sort

Practice 6 – Solution

6.1:   O(n)

6.2: $O(n^2 log n)$

This for-loop, `for (int i = 1; i <= n; i *= 2)`, generates i in this sequence: 1, 2, 4, 8, ..., so this for-loop runs $log n$ times. The two inner for-loops run n times each, so overall, these three loops run a total of $O(n^2 log n)$ times. The output of this program is 192 = 8*8*log8. The log here refers to log base 2.

6.3: $O(log n^3)$

Every for-loop in this program has Big-O of $log n$, so the Big-O of this program is $O(log n^3)$. The output of this program is 27 = log8 * log8 * log8.

6.4: $O(\sqrt{n})$

Inside the while loop, we have step = step + increment. If we expand this:
step = step + increment = 1 + 2, increment++ makes increment as 3.
step = 1 + 2 + 3
step = 1 + 2 + 3 + 4
step = 1 + 2 + 3 + 4 + ...
step = $x(x + 1)/2$ must be greater than n so that the while loop will stop.
x indicates how many times the loop is executed.
$2x^2 > x(x + 1)/2 > n$
So $x^2 > n/2$
$x > \sqrt{n/2}$
Thus, the Big-O of this program is $O(\sqrt{n}/\sqrt{2}) = O(\sqrt{n})$

6.5: $O(\sqrt{n})$

6.6:   O(n)

6.7:   0 1 2 5 3 7 4 8 6 9 11 10

6.8:   1 4 5 7 3 2 0 8 6 9 11 10

6.9:   1 3 2 0 4 5 6 7 8 9 10 11

6.10:   The ShellSort function can be implemented as:

```
void ShellSort(int Arr[], int n)
{
    bool atLeastOneSwap;
    for (int delta = n / 2; delta >= 1; delta /= 2)
    {
        do {
            atLeastOneSwap = false;
            for (int i = 0; (i + delta) < n; i++)
            {
                if (Arr[i] > Arr[i + delta])
                {
                    swap(Arr[i], Arr[i + delta]);
                    atLeastOneSwap = true;
                }
            }
        } while (atLeastOneSwap);
    }
}
```

6.11: The partition function can be implemented as:

```
int Partition(int a[], int low, int high)
{
    int pi = low;
    int pivot = a[low];
    do {
        while (low <= high && a[low] <= pivot)
            low++;
        while (a[high] > pivot)
            high--;
        if (low < high)
            swap(a[low], a[high]);
    } while (low < high);
    swap(a[pi], a[high]);
    pi = high;
    return (pi);
}
```

6.12: The MergeSort function can be implemented as:

```
void MergeSort(int Arr[], int left, int right)
{
    if (left < right)
    {
        int middle = left + (right - right) / 2;
        MergeSort(Arr, left, middle);
        MergeSort(Arr, middle + 1, right);
        merge(Arr + left, middle - left + 1, right - middle);
    }
}
```

6.13: (1)(3)(4)

6.14: (2)(3)(4)

6.15: (3)(4)

6.16: (1)

6.17: (3)

Practice Midterm 2

Problem #	Maximal Possible Points	Received
1	10	
2.1	10	
2.2	10	
2.3	10	
2.4	10	
3	10	
4	5	
5 (Optional)	0	
Total	65	

Problem #1: Stack is a LIFO (Last In First Out) container while Queue is a FIFO (First In First Out) container. If you were given 2 sequence of numbers in which the first sequence of numbers are the numbers entering a mystery container, and the second sequence of numbers are the numbers leaving a container, are you able to determine whether that mystery container is a Stack, Queue, Might Be Either One, or Neither?

For example, if you were given these two sequences:

1   2   3   // 1 entered the container first, then 2, and finally 3.

3   2   1   // 3 left the container first, then 2, and finally 1.

then that mystery container must be a Stack.

Implement the functions on the next page (which are called by the main routine on the page after that) so that this input:

10	*the number of values in test case #1*
1 2 3 4 5 6 7 8 9 10	*the values entered into the container for test #1*
10 9 8 7 6 5 4 3 2 1	*the values leaving the container for test #1*
5	*the number of values in test case #2*
1 2 3 4 5	*etc.*
1 2 3 4 5	
7	
1 2 3 4 3 2 1	
1 2 3 4 3 2 1	
4	
1 3 4 2	
1 4 2 3	

produces this output:

This is a Stack!

This is a Queue!

Either a Stack or a Queue!

Neither a Stack nor a Queue!

121

```cpp
#include <iostream>
#include <vector>
using namespace std;

bool isQueue(const vector<int>& seq1, const vector<int>& seq2)
{




















}

bool isStack(const vector<int>& seq1, const vector<int>& seq2)
{
```

```cpp
int main()
{
    int numberOfValues;

    while (cin >> numberOfValues)   // leave loop if there is no next test case
    {
        vector<int> v1, v2;

        for (int i = 0; i < numberOfValues; i++) {
            int value;
            cin >> value;
            v1.push_back(value);
        }

        for (int i = 0; i < numberOfValues; i++) {
            int value;
            cin >> value;
            v2.push_back(value);
        }

        bool s = isStack(v1, v2);
        bool q = isQueue(v1, v2);

        if (s) {
            if (q)
                cout << "Either a Stack or a Queue!" << endl;
            else
                cout << "This is a Stack!" << endl;
        }
        else {
            if (q)
                cout << "This is a Queue!" << endl;
            else
                cout << "Neither a Stack nor a Queue!" << endl;
        }
    }
}
```

Problem #2: Below is an implementation of a singly linked list with no dummy node.

```cpp
#include <iostream>
using namespace std;

class LinkedList
{
public:
    LinkedList(): head(nullptr) { }
    ~LinkedList();
    void append(int value);        // append value to the list
    void print() const;            // show the items in the list
    void printReverse() const;     // show the items in the list in the opposite order
    void reverse();                // change list so items are in the opposite order
    int sum() const;               // return the sum of the values in the list
private:
    struct Node
    {
        int num;
        Node* next;
    };
    Node* head;    // this is the only data member; do not add any others

    void printReverseHelper(const Node* p) const;
    Node* reverseHelper(Node* current, Node* previous);
    int sumHelper(const Node* p) const;
    void removeNodes(Node* p);
};

int main()
{
    LinkedList list;
    cout << list.sum() << endl;        // writes 0
    int values[4] = { 30, 10, 40, 20 };
    for (int i = 0; i < 4; i++)
        list.append(values[i]);
    list.print();                      // writes   30 10 40 20
    cout << list.sum() << endl;        // writes   100
    list.printReverse();               // writes   20 40 10 30
    list.print();                      // writes   30 10 40 20 (list wasn't changed)
    list.reverse();                    // this changes the list
    list.print();                      // writes   20 40 10 30
}
```

```cpp
void LinkedList::append(int value)
{
    Node* current = new Node;
    current->num = value;
    current->next = nullptr;
    if (head == nullptr)
        head = current;
    else {
        Node* ptr = head;
        while (ptr->next != nullptr)
            ptr = ptr->next;
        ptr->next = current;
    }
}


void LinkedList::print() const
{
    for (const Node* ptr = head; ptr != nullptr; ptr = ptr->next)
        cout << ptr->num << " ";
    cout << endl;
}
```

Problem #2.1: Please fill in the following blanks to complete the implementations of printReverse() and printReverseHelper() to print the list elements in reverse order **recursively**.

```cpp
void LinkedList::printReverse() const
{
    printReverseHelper( _____ );
    cout << endl;
}


void LinkedList::printReverseHelper(const Node* p) const
{
    if ( _____ )
        return ;

    printReverseHelper( _____ );

    cout << _____ << " ";
}
```

125

Problem #2.2: Please fill in the following blanks to complete the implementations of reverse() and reverseHelper() to reverse the linked list **recursively**.

```
void LinkedList::reverse()
{
     head = reverseHelper(head, _____ );
}
LinkedList::Node* LinkedList::reverseHelper(Node* current, Node* previous)
{
     if ( _____ )
          return previous;
     Node* last_node = reverseHelper(current->next, _____ );

     current->next = _____ ;

     return _____ ;
}
```

Problem #2.3: Please fill in the following blanks to complete the implementation of sumHelper() to compute the sum of the values in the list **recursively**.

```
int LinkedList::sum() const
{
     return sumHelper(head);
}
int LinkedList::sumHelper(const Node* p) const
{



}
```

Problem #2.4: Please fill in the following blanks to complete the implementation of removeNodes() to correctly implement the destructor **recursively**.

```
LinkedList::~LinkedList()
{
     removeNodes(head);
}

void LinkedList::removeNodes(Node* p)
{



}
```

Problem #3: Please fill in the missing blanks and code blocks below so that the output of this program is:
Base Homer Simpson
Derived Doctor Beverly Crusher
Derived Doctor Who

```
#include <iostream>
#include <vector>
#include <string>
using namespace std;

class Base
{
public:
    Base (string nm): name(nm) {}
    string getName() const { return name; }
    virtual void printName() const { cout << "Base " << name << endl; }
private:
    string name;
};

class Derived : public Base
{
public:
    Derived (string nm): Base( _____ ) {}
    virtual void printName() { cout << "Derived " << getName() << endl; }
};

void printAll(const vector<Base*>& vec)
{
    for (int i = 0; i != vec.size(); i++)    // fill in the body of the loop


        _____
};

int main() {
    vector<Base*> v;
    v.push_back(new Base("Homer Simpson"));
    v.push_back(new Derived("Beverly Crusher"));
    v.push_back(new Derived("Who"));
    printAll(v);
    for (int i = 0; i < 3; i++)
        delete _____ ;
}
```

Problem #4: You and your friends got caught by 200 cannibals (again!?). After you fought bravely for your lives, the cannibals agree that they will stop attacking you if you can answer this question: Given unlimited water and any 2 jugs (jug A and jug B with different capacity), is it possible to come up with X gallons of water in either of the jugs in 9 steps? For example, if jug A has a 3 gallon capacity and jug B can hold 5 gallons, is it possible to come up with exactly 4 gallons of water (in jug B, of course, since jug A can hold only 3 gallons)? Although you suspect that these cannibals have watched "Diehard X" before, you decided to write a program to solve it first. Fortunately, you have your old friend, your laptop, with you with the following code fragments. Now you just need to complete the code fragments and you will be free.

Sample Input:
3   5   4
7   10   2
Sample Output:
This can be solved!
This cannot be solved within 9 steps!

If you do not know why 3 5 4 is doable within 9 steps, the steps are as below:

Fill B	// A: 0	B: 5
Pour from B to A	// A: 3	B: 2
Empty A	// A: 0	B: 2
Pour from B to A	// A: 2	B: 0
Fill B	// A: 2	B: 5
Pour from B to A	// A: 3	B: 4 ← Jug B now has 4 gallons.

```cpp
#include <iostream>
#include <algorithm> // defines int min(int a, int b); returns the minimum of a and b
using namespace std;

bool isDoable(int jug1, int cap1, int jug2, int cap2, int target, int depth);

int main()
{
    int jug1_capacity, jug2_capacity, target;

    cin >> jug1_capacity >> jug2_capacity >> target;

    if (isDoable(0, jug1_capacity, 0, jug2_capacity, target, 0))
        cout << "This can be solved!" << endl;
    else
        cout << "This cannot be solved within 9 steps!" << endl;
}
```

```
bool isDoable(int jug1, int cap1, int jug2, int cap2, int target, int depth)
{
      if (jug1 == target || jug2 == target)
            return true;

      if (depth == 9)    // our limit on the depth of a recursion
            return false;

      // Can you solve it by filling A first?
      if (isDoable(cap1, cap1, jug2, cap2, target, depth+1))
            return true;

      // Can you solve it by filling B first?

      if ( _____ )
            return true;

      // Can you solve it by emptying A first?
      if (isDoable(0, cap1, jug2, cap2, target, depth+1))
            return true;

      // Can you solve it by emptying B first?

      if ( _____ )
            return true;

      // Can you solve it by pouring from B to A first?
      int amt = min(cap1 – jug1, jug2);   // unused capacity in A, or all of what's in B
      if (isDoable(jug1 + amt, cap1, jug2 - amt, cap2, target,depth+1))
            return true;

      // Can you solve it by pouring from A to B first?

      _____

      if ( _____ )

      _____

      // Nothing leads to a solution

      _____

}
```

Problem #5 (Optional): After you solved the above water jug problem, these 200 cannibals refused to honor their promises to free you guys because during the process of setting up and solving the water jug problem, both sides used too much water (apparently water is not unlimited). They want you guys to count the number of lakes around this area so that these cannibals can obtain sufficient amount of water. If you guys can complete this task, they will free you guys … (hopefully)

A lake is connected by tunnels in 8 directions as the following:

(-1 , -1)*	(-1 , 0)*	(-1, -1)*
(0 , -1)*	(0 , 0)	(0 , 1)*
(1 , -1)*	(1 , 0)*	(1 , 1)*

* indicates where (0,0) is connected to.

Thus, the map below should:

```
. . . . . . . . . .
LLL. . . . . . .
L.L. . . . . . .
.L. . . . . . . .
. . . .LL. . . .
. . . . . . . . .L
. . . .L.L.L.
L. . .LLLLL.
L. . . .LL. . .
L. . . .L. . . .
```

Show that there are 4 lakes.

```
. . . . . . . . . .
111. . . . . . .
1.1. . . . . . .
.1. . . . . . . .
. . . .22. . . .
. . . . . . . . .3
. . . .3.3.3.
4. . .33333.
4. . . .33. . .
4. . . .3. . . .
```

Fortunately, you have your laptop with you with code fragments. All you need to do is to fill in the blanks and you should be free from these cannibals.

```cpp
#include <iostream>
using namespace std;

void search(char field[10][11], int x,int y,int N,int M, char fill)
{
    if( x < 0 || y < 0 || x >= N || y >= M || field[x][y] != 'L' )
        return ;

    field[x][y] = fill;

    // Could be 8 lines of codes below (or 3 lines by using for-loops...)




















}

int solve_it(char field[10][11],int N, int M)
{
    int count = 0;
    for(int i = 0; i < N ; i++ )
        for(int j = 0; j < M ; j++)
        {
            if(field[i][j] == 'L')
            {
                count++;
                search(field,i,j,N,M,count+'0');
            }
        }
    return count;
}
```

```cpp
int main()
{
    char field[10][11] = {
        "..........",
        "LLL.......",
        "L.L.......",
        ".L........",
        "....LL....",
        ".........L",
        "....L.L.L.",
        "L...LLLLL.",
        "L....LL...",
        "L....L...." };

    for(int q=0;q<10;q++)
        cout << field[q] << endl;

    cout << "There are " << solve_it(field, 10, 10) << " lakes" << endl;

    for(int q=0;q<10;q++)
        cout << field[q] << endl;

}
```

Practice Midterm 2 – Solution

1:   The isQueue and isStack functions can be implemented as:

```cpp
bool isQueue(const vector<int>& seq1, const vector<int>& seq2)
{
    for (int i = 0; i < seq1.size(); i++)
        if (seq1[i] != seq2[i])
            return false;
    return true;
}
bool isStack(const vector<int>& seq1, const vector<int>& seq2)
{
    for (int i = 0; i < seq1.size(); i++)
        if (seq1[i] != seq2[seq2.size() - i - 1])
            return false;
    return true;
}
```

2.1:   The printReverse and printReverseHelper member functions can be implemented as:

```cpp
void LinkedList::printReverse() const
{
    printReverseHelper(head);
    cout << endl;
}
void LinkedList::printReverseHelper(const Node* p) const
{
    if (p == nullptr)
        return;

    printReverseHelper(p->next);

    cout << p->num << " ";
}
```

2.2:   The reverse and reverseHelper member functions can be implemented as:

```cpp
void LinkedList::reverse()
{
    head = reverseHelper(head, nullptr);
}
LinkedList::Node*
LinkedList::reverseHelper(Node* current, Node* previous)
{
    if (current == nullptr)
        return previous;
    Node* last_node = reverseHelper(current->next, current);
    current->next = previous;
    return last_node;
}
```

2.3: The sum and sumHelper member functions can be implemented as:

```
int LinkedList::sum() const
{
    return sumHelper(head);
}
int LinkedList::sumHelper(const Node* p) const
{
    if (p == nullptr)
        return 0;
    return p->num + sumHelper(p->next);
}
```

2.4: The destructor and removeNodes member function can be implemented as:

```
LinkedList::~LinkedList()
{
    removeNodes(head);
}
void LinkedList::removeNodes(Node* p)
{
    if (p == nullptr)
        return;
    removeNodes(p->next);
    delete p;
}
```

3:
```
class Base
{
public:
    Base(string nm) : name(nm) {}
    string getName() const { return name; }
    virtual void printName() const { cout << "Base " << name << endl; }
private:
    string name;
};

class Derived : public Base
{
public:
    Derived(string nm) : Base("Doctor " + nm) { }
    virtual void printName() { cout << "Derived " << getName() <<
endl; }
};

void printAll(const vector<Base*>& vec)
{
    for (int i = 0; i != vec.size(); i++)// fill in the body of the loop
        vec[i]->printName();            // or (*vec[i]).printName();
};

int main()
{
    vector<Base*> v;
    v.push_back(new Base("Homer Simpson"));
    v.push_back(new Derived("Beverly Crusher"));
    v.push_back(new Derived("Who"));
    printAll(v);
    for (int i = 0; i < 3; i++)
        delete v[i];
}
```

4:
```
bool isDoable(int jug1,int cap1,int jug2,int cap2,int target,int depth)
{
    if (jug1 == target || jug2 == target)
        return true;

    if (depth == 9)  // our limit on the depth of a recursion
        return false;

    // Can you solve it by filling A first?
    if (isDoable(cap1, cap1, jug2, cap2, target, depth + 1))
        return true;

    // Can you solve it by filling B first?
    if (isDoable(jug1, cap1, cap2, cap2, target, depth + 1))
        return true;

    // Can you solve it by emptying A first?
    if (isDoable(0, cap1, jug2, cap2, target, depth + 1))
        return true;

    // Can you solve it by emptying B first?
    if (isDoable(jug1, cap1, 0, cap2, target, depth + 1))
        return true;

    // Can you solve it by pouring from B to A first?
    int amt = min(cap1 - jug1, jug2);  // unused capacity in A,
                                       // or all of what's in B
    if (isDoable(jug1 + amt, cap1, jug2 - amt, cap2, target, depth + 1))
        return true;

    // Can you solve it by pouring from A to B first?
    amt = min(jug1, cap2 - jug2);
    if (isDoable(jug1 - amt, cap1, jug2 + amt, cap2, target, depth + 1))
        return true;

    // Nothing leads to a solution
    return false;
}
```
5:
```
void search(char field[10][11], int x, int y, int N, int M, char fill)
{
    if (x < 0 || y < 0 || x >= N || y >= M || field[x][y] != 'L')
        return;
    field[x][y] = fill;
    // Could be 8 lines of codes below (or 3 lines by using for-loops...)
    search(field, x - 1, y - 1, N, M, fill);
    search(field, x - 1, y, N, M, fill);
    search(field, x - 1, y + 1, N, M, fill);
    search(field, x, y - 1, N, M, fill);
    search(field, x, y + 1, N, M, fill);
    search(field, x + 1, y - 1, N, M, fill);
    search(field, x + 1, y, N, M, fill);
    search(field, x + 1, y + 1, N, M, fill);
    // or
    // for(int i = -1 ; i <= 1; i++ )
    //     for(int j = -1 ; j <= 1 ; j++ )
    //         search(field,x + i , y + j, N, M, fill);
}
```

135

Practice 7 – Trees

Problem 7.1: Given the following Binary Search Tree class definition, please answer questions starting from Problem #7.1.1.

```cpp
#include <iostream>
#include <queue>
using namespace std;
struct Node {
    Node(const int &myVal) {
        value = myVal;
        left = right = nullptr;
    }
    int value;
    Node *left,*right;
};
class BinarySearchTree {
public:
    BinarySearchTree() { m_root = nullptr; }
    ~BinarySearchTree() { FreeTree(m_root); }
    Node* getRoot() { return m_root; }

    void insert(const int value);
    void preorder(Node *ptr);
    void inorder(Node *ptr);
    void postorder(Node *ptr);
    void levelorder();
    int GetMin(Node *pRoot);
    int GetMax(Node *pRoot);
    bool Search(int V,Node *ptr);
private:
    Node *m_root;
    void FreeTree(Node *cur);
};
int main() {
    BinarySearchTree BST;
    BST.insert(5); BST.insert(3); BST.insert(7);
    for(int i = 0 ; i <= 10 ; i += 2 )
        BST.insert(i); // Insert 0, 2, 4, 6, 8, 10

    BST.preorder (BST.getRoot());   cout << endl;
    BST.inorder   (BST.getRoot());   cout << endl;
    BST.postorder(BST.getRoot());   cout << endl;
    BST.levelorder(); cout << endl;
    cout << "Minimal value is: " << BST.GetMin( BST.getRoot() ) << endl;
    cout << "Maximal value is: " << BST.GetMax( BST.getRoot() ) << endl;
}
```

// The outputs of the program are:
5 3 0 2 4 7 6 8 10
0 2 3 4 5 6 7 8 10
2 0 4 3 6 10 8 7 5
5 3 7 0 4 6 8 2 10
Minimal value is: 0
Maximal value is: 10

Problem #7.1.1: Please draw the Binary Search Tree after all inserts are completed.

Problem #7.1.2: Please write the implementation of FreeTree().

```
void BinarySearchTree::FreeTree(Node *cur) {
    if (cur == nullptr)
        return;




}
```

Problem #7.1.3: Please write the implementation of insert().

```
void BinarySearchTree::insert(const int value)
{
    if (m_root == nullptr)
    {
        m_root = new Node(value);
        return;
    }
    Node *cur = m_root;
    for (;;)
    {
        if (value == cur->value)
            return;
        if (value < cur->value)
        {
            if (cur->left != nullptr)


                _____
            else {

                _____
                return;
            }
        }
        else if (value > cur->value)
        {
            if (cur->right != nullptr)


                _____
            else {

                _____
                return;
            }
        }
    }
}
```

Problem #7.1.4: Please write the implementation of preorder().

```cpp
void BinarySearchTree::preorder(Node *ptr)
{
    if(ptr == nullptr)
        return ;
    cout << ptr->value << " ";


    _____


    _____

}
```

Problem #7.1.5: Please write the implementation of inorder().

```cpp
void BinarySearchTree::inorder(Node *ptr)
{
    if(ptr == nullptr)
        return ;

    _____
    cout << ptr->value << " ";

    _____

}
```

Problem #7.1.6: Please write the implementation of postorder().

```cpp
void BinarySearchTree::postorder(Node *ptr)
{
    if(ptr== nullptr)
        return ;


    _____


    _____
    cout << ptr->value << " ";
}
```

Problem #7.1.7: Please write the implementation of Search().

```cpp
bool BinarySearchTree::Search(int V, Node *ptr)
{
    if(ptr == nullptr )
        return false;
    if(V == ptr->value)
        return true;
    else if(V < ptr->value)
        return Search(_____);
    else
        return Search(_____);
}
```

139

```
void BinarySearchTree::levelorder()
{
    if (m_root == nullptr) return ;
    queue<Node*> q;
    q.push(m_root);
    while( ! q.empty() ) {
        Node *visited_node = q.front();
        q.pop();
        if(visited_node->left != nullptr )


        _____


        if(visited_node->right!= nullptr )


        _____


        cout << visited_node->value << " ";
    }
}
```

```
int BinarySearchTree::GetMin(Node *pRoot)
{
    if (pRoot == nullptr)
        return(-1);   // empty

    while (pRoot->left != nullptr)


    _____


    return(_____);
}

int BinarySearchTree::GetMax(Node *pRoot)
{
    if (pRoot == nullptr)
        return(-1);   // empty

    while (_____)


    _____


    return(pRoot->value);
}
```

Problem #7.2: If we change the main() function in problem #7.1 as the following, what is the output then? Please also draw the binary search tree.

```
int main()
{
    BinarySearchTree BST;

    BST.insert(0); BST.insert(1); BST.insert(2);
    for(int i = 3 ; i <= 10 ; i += 2 )
        BST.insert(i);  // Insert 3, 5, 7, 9

    BST.preorder (BST.getRoot());    cout << endl;
    BST.inorder   (BST.getRoot());   cout << endl;
    BST.postorder(BST.getRoot());    cout << endl;
    BST.levelorder(); cout << endl;

    cout << "Minimal value is: " << BST.GetMin( BST.getRoot() ) << endl;
    cout << "Maximal value is: " << BST.GetMax( BST.getRoot() ) << endl;
}
```

Problem #7.3: Suppose we added the following new member functions into the BinarySearchTree class definition in Problem #7.1 and a new main() function. The outputs of the following program are:

Size of BST is: 9
Height of BST is: 4
There are 4 leaf nodes
There are 5 non-leaf nodes
Sum of all nodes is: 45
There is a path sum of 18

```cpp
class BinarySearchTree
{
public:
    // Same constructors, insert ... etc as in problem #7.1.
    int size(Node *ptr);
    int height(Node *ptr);
    int numOfLeafNodes(Node *ptr);
    int numOfNonLeafNodes(Node *ptr);
    int sumOfAllNodes(Node *ptr);
    bool hasPathSum(Node *ptr,int sum);
    void reflectBinaryTree(Node* current);
private:
    // Same private member functions as in problem #7.1.
};
int main()
{
    BinarySearchTree BST;

    BST.insert(5); BST.insert(3); BST.insert(7);
    for(int i = 0 ; i <= 10 ; i += 2 )
        BST.insert(i); // Insert 0, 2, 4, 6, 8, 10

    cout << "Size of BST is: " << BST.size( BST.getRoot() ) << endl;
    cout << "Height of BST is: " << BST.height( BST.getRoot() ) << endl;
    cout << "There are " << BST.numOfLeafNodes( BST.getRoot() )
        << " leaf nodes " << endl;
    cout << "There are " << BST.numOfNonLeafNodes( BST.getRoot() )
        << " non-leaf nodes " << endl;
    cout << "Sum of all nodes is: " << BST.sumOfAllNodes(BST.getRoot() )
        << endl;

    if( BST.hasPathSum( BST.getRoot(), 4 ) )
        cout << "There is a path sum of 4" << endl;
    if( BST.hasPathSum( BST.getRoot(), 18 ) )
        cout << "There is a path sum of 18" << endl;

}
```

142

```
int BinarySearchTree::size(Node *ptr)
{
    if(ptr == nullptr)
        return 0;

    return _____
}
```

```
int BinarySearchTree::sumOfAllNodes(Node *ptr)
{
    if(ptr == nullptr)
        return 0;

    return _____
}
```

```
int BinarySearchTree::height(Node *ptr)
{
    if(ptr == nullptr)
        return 0;

    int left_height = _____

    int right_height = _____

    if( _____ )

        return _____
    else

        return _____
}
```

143

Problem #7.3.4: Please implement the numOfLeafNodes() member function.

```
int BinarySearchTree::numOfLeafNodes(Node *ptr)
{
    if(ptr == nullptr)
        return 0;

    if( _____ )
        return 1;

    return _____
}
```

Problem #7.3.5: Please implement the numOfNonLeafNodes() member function.

```
int BinarySearchTree::numOfNonLeafNodes(Node *ptr)
{
    if(ptr == nullptr || ( _____ ))
        return 0;

    return _____
}
```

Problem #7.3.6: Please write the implementation of the hasPathSum() member function. The Path Sum is the sum of the value in each node in any path starting from the root node and ending at the leaf node. Every value is assumed to be positive in every node. This member function returns true if there is a specific path sum, otherwise return false.

```
bool BinarySearchTree::hasPathSum(Node *ptr, int sum)
{
    if( ptr == nullptr && sum == 0)
        _____

    if( ptr == nullptr && sum != 0)

        _____

    return hasPathSum( _____ ) ||

        hasPathSum( _____ );
}
```

Problem #7.3.7: Please write the implementation of the reflectBinaryTree() member function so that the outputs of the following main function are:
5 7 3 8 6 4 0 10 2
5 7 8 10 6 3 4 0 2
The reflectBinaryTree() member function reflects a binary tree by swapping the left and right children of each node.

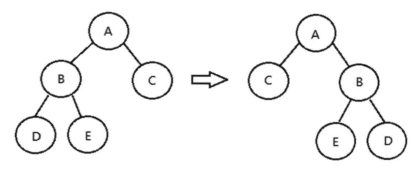

```cpp
void BinarySearchTree::reflectBinaryTree(Node* current)
{
    Node *temp;
    if (current != nullptr)
    {



    }
}

int main()
{
    BinarySearchTree BST;

    BST.insert(5); BST.insert(3); BST.insert(7);
    for (int i = 0; i <= 10; i += 2) BST.insert(i);
    BST.reflectBinaryTree(BST.getRoot());
    BST.levelorder();                   cout << endl;
    BST.preorder(BST.getRoot());        cout << endl;
}
```

Problem #7.3.8: In Problem #7.3.7, you reflected a binary tree. This problem concerns about verifying whether one binary tree is the reflection of another binary tree. Please fill in the blanks for the isReflection() function by calling isReflection() recursively. If we call isReflection(root1,root2) where root1 is the root node of the first binary tree and root2 is the root node of the second binary tree, then the isReflection() function returns true if the first binary tree is the inversion of the second binary tree; otherwise, it returns false. The outputs of the following program should be: *BST_A is the reflection of BST_B!*

```cpp
bool isReflection(Node *curr1, Node *curr2)
{

        if (curr1 == nullptr && curr2 == nullptr)


        _____


        if (curr1 && curr2)
        {
            return _____ &&

                   _____ &&

                   _____ ;

        }
        else
            return false;
}
int main()
{
    BinarySearchTree BST_A, BST_B;

    BST_A.insert(5); BST_A.insert(3); BST_A.insert(7);
    for (int i = 0; i <= 10; i += 2)
        BST_A.insert(i);

    BST_B.insert(5); BST_B.insert(3); BST_B.insert(7);
    for (int i = 0; i <= 10; i += 2)
        BST_B.insert(i);
    BST_B.reflectBinaryTree(BST_B.getRoot());

    if (isReflection(BST_A.getRoot(), BST_B.getRoot()))
        cout << "BST_A is the reflection of BST_B!" << endl;
    else
        cout << "BST_A is NOT the reflection of BST_B!" << endl;

}
```

Problem #7.4: Which of the followings are **TRUE**?

(1) If we use in-order traversal on any binary tree (each of the node has an integer value), the resulting numbers are always sorted.

(2) If we use in-order traversal on any binary search tree (each of the node has an integer value), the resulting numbers are always sorted.

(3) If we use pre-order traversal on any binary search tree (each of the node has an integer value), the resulting numbers are always sorted.

(4) There exists a binary tree such that the in-order, pre-order, post-order, and level-order traversals all give the same output.

(5) If all the nodes in a binary tree do not have the right child node, then the outputs from in-order and post-order traversals are the same.

(6) If all the nodes in a binary tree do not have the right child node, then the outputs from pre-order and post-order traversals are the same.

(7) If all the nodes in a binary tree do not have the right child node, then the outputs from pre-order and in-order traversals are the same.

(8) If all the nodes in a binary tree do not have the left child node, then the outputs from in-order and post-order traversals are the same.

(9) If all the nodes in a binary tree do not have the left child node, then the outputs from pre-order and post-order traversals are the same.

(10) If all the nodes in a binary tree do not have the left child node, then the outputs from pre-order and in-order traversals are the same.

(11) If a binary tree is empty, then the outputs from pre-order, in-order, post-order, and level-order traversals are the same.

(12) The maximum number of leaf nodes at the L-th level in a binary tree is 2^{L-1} assuming the root node is at Level 1.

(13) In a binary tree, assume P is the number of leaf nodes, and Q is the number of nodes that have 2 children. Then it's ALWAYS the case that P = Q + 2.

Practice 7 – Solution

7.1.1:

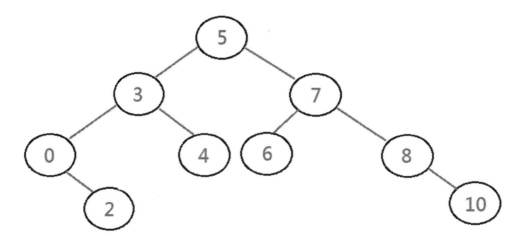

7.1.2: The FreeTree member function can be implemented as:

```cpp
void BinarySearchTree::FreeTree(Node *cur) {
    if (cur == nullptr)
        return;
    FreeTree(cur->left);
    FreeTree(cur->right);
    delete cur;
}
```

7.1.3: The insert member function can be implemented as:

```cpp
void BinarySearchTree::insert(const int value) {
    if (m_root == nullptr) {
        m_root = new Node(value);
        return;
    }
    Node *cur = m_root;
    for (;;) {
        if (value == cur->value)
            return;
        if (value < cur->value) {
            if (cur->left != nullptr)
                cur = cur->left;
            else {
                cur->left = new Node(value);
                return;
            }
        }
        else if (value > cur->value) {
            if (cur->right != nullptr)
                cur = cur->right;
            else {
                cur->right = new Node(value);
                return;
            }
        }
    }
}
```

7.1.4: The preorder member function can be implemented as:
```cpp
void BinarySearchTree::preorder(Node *ptr) {
    if (ptr == nullptr)
        return;
    cout << ptr->value << " ";
    preorder(ptr->left);
    preorder(ptr->right);
}
```

7.1.5: The inorder member function can be implemented as:
```cpp
void BinarySearchTree::inorder(Node *ptr) {
    if (ptr == nullptr)
        return;
    inorder(ptr->left);
    cout << ptr->value << " ";
    inorder(ptr->right);
}
```

7.1.6: The postorder member function can be implemented as:
```cpp
void BinarySearchTree::postorder(Node *ptr) {
    if (ptr == nullptr)
        return;
    postorder(ptr->left);
    postorder(ptr->right);
    cout << ptr->value << " ";
}
```

7.1.7: The search member function can be implemented as:
```cpp
bool BinarySearchTree::Search(int V, Node *ptr) {
    if (ptr == nullptr)
        return false;
    if (V == ptr->value)
        return true;
    else if (V < ptr->value)
        return Search(V, ptr->left);
    else
        return Search(V, ptr->right);
}
```

7.1.8: The levelorder member function can be implemented as:
```cpp
void BinarySearchTree::levelorder() {
    if (m_root == nullptr) return;
    queue<Node*> q;
    q.push(m_root);
    while (!q.empty()) {
        Node *visited_node = q.front();
        q.pop();
        if (visited_node->left != nullptr)
            q.push(visited_node->left);
        if (visited_node->right != nullptr)
            q.push(visited_node->right);
        cout << visited_node->value << " ";
    }
}
```

7.1.9: The GetMin and GetMax member functions can be implemented as:

```
int BinarySearchTree::GetMin(Node *pRoot) {
    if (pRoot == nullptr)
        return(-1); // empty
    while (pRoot->left != nullptr)
        pRoot = pRoot->left;
    return pRoot->value;
}
int BinarySearchTree::GetMax(Node *pRoot) {
    if (pRoot == nullptr)
        return(-1); // empty
    while (pRoot->right != nullptr)
        pRoot = pRoot->right;
    return(pRoot->value);
}
```

7.2: The outputs from this program are:

0 1 2 3 5 7 9
0 1 2 3 5 7 9
9 7 5 3 2 1 0
0 1 2 3 5 7 9
Minimal value is: 0
Maximal value is: 9

The binary search tree looks like this:

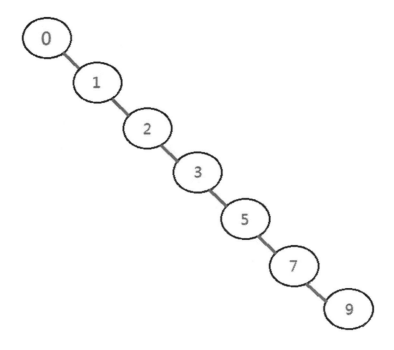

7.3.1: The size member function can be implemented as:

```
int BinarySearchTree::size(Node *ptr)
{
    if (ptr == nullptr)
        return 0;
    return 1 + size(ptr->left) + size(ptr->right);
}
```

150

7.3.2: The sumOfAllNodes member function can be implemented as:

```
int BinarySearchTree::sumOfAllNodes(Node *ptr)
{
    if (ptr == nullptr)
        return 0;
    return ptr->value +
            sumOfAllNodes(ptr->left) +
            sumOfAllNodes(ptr->right);
}
```

7.3.3: The height member function can be implemented as:

```
int BinarySearchTree::height(Node *ptr)
{
    if (ptr == nullptr)
        return 0;
    int left_height = height(ptr->left);
    int right_height = height(ptr->right);
    if (left_height > right_height)
        return left_height + 1;
    else
        return right_height + 1;
}
```

7.3.4: The numOfLeafNodes member function can be implemented as:

```
int BinarySearchTree::numOfLeafNodes(Node *ptr)
{
    if (ptr == nullptr)
        return 0;
    if (ptr->left == nullptr && ptr->right == nullptr)
        return 1;
    return numOfLeafNodes(ptr->left) + numOfLeafNodes(ptr->right);
}
```

7.3.5: The numOfNonLeafNodes member function can be implemented as:

```
int BinarySearchTree::numOfNonLeafNodes(Node *ptr)
{
    if (ptr==nullptr || (ptr->left == nullptr && ptr->right == nullptr))
        return 0;
    return 1+numOfNonLeafNodes(ptr->left)+numOfNonLeafNodes(ptr->right);
}
```

7.3.6: The hasPathSum member function can be implemented as:

```
bool BinarySearchTree::hasPathSum(Node *ptr, int sum)
{
    if (ptr == nullptr && sum == 0)
        return true;
    if (ptr == nullptr && sum != 0)
        return false;
    return hasPathSum(ptr->left, sum - ptr->value) ||
        hasPathSum(ptr->right, sum - ptr->value);
}
```

7.3.7: The reflectBinaryTree member function can be implemented as:

```
void BinarySearchTree::reflectBinaryTree(Node* current)
{
    Node *temp;
    if (current != nullptr) {
        reflectBinaryTree(current->left);
        reflectBinaryTree(current->right);
        temp = current->left;
        current->left = current->right;
        current->right = temp;
    }
}
```

7.3.8: The isReflection member function can be implemented as:

```
bool isReflection(Node *curr1, Node *curr2)
{

    if (curr1 == nullptr && curr2 == nullptr)
        return true;

    if (curr1 && curr2) {
        return (curr1->value == curr2->value) &&
            isReflection(curr1->left, curr2->right) &&
            isReflection(curr1->right, curr2->left);
    }
    else
        return false;
}
```

7.4: (2)(4)(5)(10)(11)(12)

Practice 8 – Hash Tables and Heap

Problem #8.1: Below is an implementation of a Closed Hash Table. Please fill in the blanks so that the outputs of this program are:
10 11 12 13 14 15 16 17 -1 -1
no room left in hash table!!!
no room left in hash table!!!
10 11 12 13 14 15 16 17 20 21

```
#include <iostream>
using namespace std;
#define NUM_BUCK      10

class ClosedHashTable
{
public:
      void insert(int idNum);
      bool search(int idNum) const;
      void output() const;
private:
      inline int hashFunc(int idNum) const
      {
            return idNum % NUM_BUCK;
      }
      struct BUCKET
      {
            int idNum;
            bool used;
            BUCKET() { used = false; idNum = -1; }
      };
      BUCKET m_buckets[NUM_BUCK];
};

int main()
{
      ClosedHashTable cht;

      for (int i = 0; i<8; i++)
            cht.insert(i + 10);       // Insert 10, 11, 12, 13, 14, 15, 16, 17
      cht.output();

      for (int i = 0; i<4; i++)       // Insert 20, 21, 22, and 23
            cht.insert(i + 20);
      cht.output();

      if (cht.search(23))
            cout << "23 is in the hash table." << endl;
}
```

153

```cpp
void ClosedHashTable::insert(int idNum)
{
    int bucket = hashFunc( _____ );
    for (int tries = 0; tries<NUM_BUCK; tries++)
    {
        if (m_buckets[bucket].used == false)
        {
            m_buckets[bucket].idNum = _____;
            m_buckets[bucket].used = _____;
            return;
        }
        bucket = (bucket + 1) % _____ ;
    }
    cout << "no room left in hash table!!!" << endl;
}
bool ClosedHashTable::search(int idNum) const
{
    int bucket = hashFunc(_____ );
    for (int tries = 0; tries<NUM_BUCK; tries++)
    {
        if (m_buckets[bucket].used == _____ )
            return false;
        if (m_buckets[bucket].idNum == _____ )
            return true;
        bucket = (bucket + 1) % _____;
    }
    return false;     // false means that idNum is not in the hash table.
}

void ClosedHashTable::output() const
{
    for (int i = 0; i<NUM_BUCK; i++)
        cout << m_buckets[i].idNum << " ";
    cout << endl;
}
```

Problem #8.2: Below is an implementation of an Open Hash Table. Please fill in the blanks so that the outputs of this program are:

0: 10 20
1: 11 21
2: 12 22
3: 13 23
4: 14 24
5: 15 25
6: 16 26
7: 17 27
8: 18 28
9: 19 29
----
29 is in the open hash table.

```
#include <iostream>
#include <list>
#define NUM_BUCK     10
using namespace std;

class OpenHashTable
{
public:
    void insert(int idNum);
    bool search(int idNum);
    void output();
private:
    inline int hashFunc(int idNum) const
    {
        return idNum % NUM_BUCK;
    }
    struct BUCKET
    {
        list<int> idNum;
    };
    BUCKET m_buckets[NUM_BUCK];
};
int main()
{
    OpenHashTable oht;
    for (int i = 10; i<30; i++)
        oht.insert(i);
    oht.output();
    cout << "---------------" << endl;
    if (oht.search(29))
        cout << "29 is in the open hash table." << endl;
}
```

155

```cpp
void OpenHashTable::insert(int idNum)
{
    int bucket = hashFunc(idNum);

    m_buckets[bucket].idNum.push_back(idNum);
}

bool OpenHashTable::search(int idNum)
{
    int bucket = hashFunc(idNum);

    list<int>::iterator it = m_buckets[bucket]. _____ ;

    for (;it != m_buckets[bucket]. _____ ; it++)
        if (*it == idNum)
            return true;      // idNum is in the hash table

    return false;                 // false means idNum is not in the hash table
}

void OpenHashTable::output()
{
    for (int i = 0; i < NUM_BUCK ; i++)
    {
        cout << i << ": ";

        list<int>::iterator it = m_buckets[i]. _____ ;

        for (; it != m_buckets[i]._____ ; it++)
            cout << *it << " ";
        cout << endl;
    }
}
```

Problem #8.3: Is the output of the following program sorted in ascending order?

```
#include <unordered_map>
#include <iostream>
#include <string>
using namespace std;
int main( )
{
    unordered_map <string, int> hm;
    unordered_map <string, int>::iterator iter;

    hm["D"] = 40;
    hm["C"] = 30;
    hm["A"] = 10;
    hm["B"] = 20;
    hm["E"] = 50;

    for( iter=hm.begin() ; iter != hm.end() ; iter++ )
        cout << iter->first << " " << iter->second << endl;
}
```

Problem #8.4: Which one of the following hash functions can evenly distribute these 7 numbers (7, 23, 26, 40, 42, 58, 90) into a closed hash table with only 10 slots without causing collisons? Assuming NUM is the variable representing a number from these 7 numbers.

(1) NUM % 10
(2) NUM / 10
(3) (NUM + 11) % 10
(4) (NUM + 11) / 10
(5) (NUM / 10 + NUM % 10) % 10

Problem #8.5: If an open hash table has 101 slots (from slot #0 to slot #100) that will be used to store numbers from 1 to 9999. Which one of the following hash functions does not store any values in slot #0? Assuming NUM is the variable representing a number from those 9999 numbers.

(1) (NUM % 100) + 1
(2) NUM % 101
(3) (NUM − 1) / 101
(4) (NUM + 1) % 99

Problem #8.6: Please fill in the blanks below to complete the implementation of the heap_sort function so that the outputs of this program are:
0 1 2 3 4 5 6 7 8 9

```cpp
#include <iostream>
#include <algorithm>
#include <vector>
using namespace std;

void sift_down(vector<int>& heap, int start_node, int end_node)
{
    int child_node, left, right;

    while (start_node < end_node)
    {
        child_node = start_node;

        left = (2 * start_node) + 1;

        right = left + 1;

        if (left < end_node && heap[left] > heap[child_node])
            child_node = left;

        if (right < end_node && heap[right] > heap[child_node])
            child_node = right;

        if (child_node == start_node)
            return;

        swap(heap[start_node], heap[child_node]);

        start_node = child_node;
    }
}

void make_heap(vector<int>& arr)
{
    int start_node = (arr.size() / 2) - 1;

    while (start_node >= 0)
    {
        sift_down(arr, start_node, arr.size());

        start_node--;
    }
}
```

158

```cpp
void heap_sort(vector<int>& arr)
{
    make_heap(arr);

    int end = arr.size() - 1;

    while (end > 0)
    {
        swap(arr[0], _____ );

        sift_down(arr, 0, end);

        --end;
    }
}

int main()
{
    int values[10] = { 3, 5, 7, 1, 2, 4, 6, 8, 9, 0 };

    vector<int> data(values, values + 10);

    heap_sort(data);

    for (int i = 0; i< 10; i++)
        cout << data[i] << " ";

    cout << endl;
}
```

Problem #8.7: Given a maxheap, please fill in the blanks to find the minimum element in O($\frac{N}{2}$) time. Assume we re-use the make_heap() and sift_down() functions from problem #8.6.

```cpp
int findMin(vector<int> &data)
{
    int Min;
    int end_node = (data.size() / 2) - 1;

    if (data.size() >= 1)
        Min = data[data.size() - 1];

    for ( _____ )
        if (data[i] < Min)
            Min = data[i];

    return Min;
}

int main()
{
    int values[10] = { 3, 5, 7, 1, 2, 4, 6, 8, 9, 0 };

    vector<int> data(values, values + 10);

    make_heap(data);

    cout << "Min value is: " << findMin(data) << endl;
}
```

Problem #8.8: Assume that we re-use the make_heap() and sift_down() functions from problem #8.6, please fill in the blanks to use pre-order traversal to find all the values in the heap that is less than 5 so that the outputs of this program are:
3 1 2 0 4

```
void findLessThanValue(vector<int> &data, int root, int value)
{
    if( root < data.size() )
    {

        if(data[ root ] < value)
            cout << data[root] << " ";


        _____


        _____


    }
}

int main()
{
    int values[10] = {3,5,7,1,2,4,6,8,9,0};

    vector<int> data(values,values+10);

    make_heap(data);

    findLessThanValue(data, 0, 5);

    cout << endl;
}
```

Practice 8 – Solution

8.1:   The insert and search member functions can be implemented as:

```cpp
void ClosedHashTable::insert(int idNum)
{
    int bucket = hashFunc(idNum);
    for (int tries = 0; tries<NUM_BUCK; tries++)
    {
        if (m_buckets[bucket].used == false)
        {
            m_buckets[bucket].idNum = idNum;
            m_buckets[bucket].used = true;
            return;
        }
        bucket = (bucket + 1) % NUM_BUCK;
    }
    cout << "no room left in hash table!!!" << endl;
}
bool ClosedHashTable::search(int idNum) const
{
    int bucket = hashFunc(idNum);
    for (int tries = 0; tries<NUM_BUCK; tries++)
    {
        if (m_buckets[bucket].used == false)
            return false;
        if (m_buckets[bucket].idNum == idNum)
            return true;
        bucket = (bucket + 1) % NUM_BUCK;
    }
    return false; // false means that idNum is not in the hash table.
}
```

8.2:   The search and output member functions can be implemented as:

```cpp
bool OpenHashTable::search(int idNum)
{
    int bucket = hashFunc(idNum);

    list<int>::iterator it = m_buckets[bucket].idNum.begin();

    for (;it != m_buckets[bucket].idNum.end() ; it++)
        if (*it == idNum)
            return true;  // idNum is in the hash table

    return false;         // false means idNum is not in the hash table
}
void OpenHashTable::output()
{
    for (int i = 0; i < NUM_BUCK ; i++)
    {
        cout << i << ": ";
        list<int>::iterator it = m_buckets[i].idNum.begin();
        for (; it != m_buckets[i].idNum.end() ; it++)
            cout << *it << " ";
        cout << endl;
    }
}
```

8.3: No. Hash tables do not store values in ascending/descending order.

8.4: (5)

8.5: (1)

8.6: The heap_sort function can be implemented as:

```
void heap_sort(vector<int>& arr)
{
    make_heap(arr);
    int end = arr.size() - 1;
    while (end > 0)
    {
        swap(arr[0], arr[end]);
        sift_down(arr, 0, end);
        --end;
    }
}
```

8.7: The findMin function can be implemented as:

```
int findMin(vector<int> &data)
{
    int Min;
    int end_node = (data.size() / 2) - 1;
    if (data.size() >= 1)
        Min = data[data.size() - 1];
    for(int i = data.size() - 2; i > end_node; i--)
        if (data[i] < Min)
            Min = data[i];
    return Min;
}
```

8.8: The findLessThanValue function can be implemented as:

```
void findLessThanValue(vector<int> &data, int root, int value)
{
    if (root < data.size())
    {
        if (data[root] < value)
            cout << data[root] << " ";
        findLessThanValue(data, 2 * root + 1, value);
        findLessThanValue(data, 2 * root + 2, value);
    }
}
```

Practice 9 – Graph

Problem #9.1: Show an adjacency matrix and an adjacency list for the following directed graph. In a directed graph, an edge has orientations that connects from one vertex to the other in a specific direction.

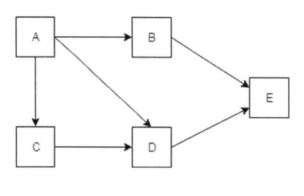

Problem #9.2: If you perform a Breadth-First traversal from vertex A in the following graph, what vertices will be visited and in what order? What about performing a Depth-First traversal?

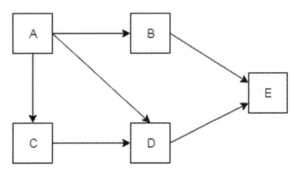

Problem #9.3: Below is an directed graph with 5 vertices and 6 edges. Each edge has a number representing the distance between two vertices. For example, the vertex A and B have a distance of 2 units. Please use Dijkstra's algorithm from vertex A and fill in the blanks in the distance array below. Each line of the distance array shows the distance from vertex A to any other nodes in the directed graph after picking an unprocessed vertex V that has the shortest distance so far, iterating through all the vertices to see if the vertex V can reach any other vertices resulting in a smaller distance. If so, update the distance in the distance array. The algorithm keeps doing this until all unprocessed vertices are processed.

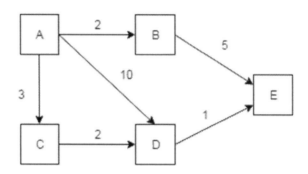

For example, the second line of the distance array shows that vertex A can go to vertex B with 2 units, vertex C with 3 units, and vertex D with 10 units, but vertex A cannot go to vertex E directly (with a distance of infinity) after using vertex A to visit its neighboring vertices. The last line of the distance array shows the shortest distance from vertex A to any other vertices. For example, the shortest distance from vertex A to vertex E is 6 units (A -> C -> D -> E). You job is to complete the following distance array at each iteration of the Dijkstra's algorithm.

A	B	C	D	E
0	2	3	10	∞
0				
0				
0	2	3	5	6

Problem #9.4: Consider the following undirected Graph:

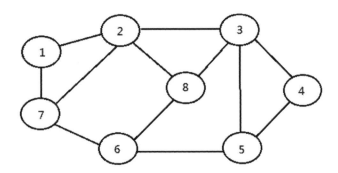

Which one of the following is correct?

(A) Starting from vertex 8, one possible sequence of node numbers generated from Breadth-First traversal is { 8, 2, 3, 6, 1, 7, 4, 5 }.

(B) Starting from vertex 3, one possible sequence of node numbers generated from Depth-First traversal is { 3, 2, 1, 7, 4, 8, 5, 6}.

(C) Starting from vertex 4, one possible sequence of node numbers generated from Breadth-First traversal is { 4, 3, 2, 1, 5, 6, 7, 8 }.

(D) Starting from vertex 1, one possible sequence of node numbers generated from Breadth-First traversal is { 1, 2, 3, 4, 5, 6, 7, 8}.

(E) Assume each edge costs 1 unit, the shortest path going from vertex 4 to vertex 7 costs 4 units.

Practice 9 – Solution

9.1: Adjacency matrix is shown below. Row is source and column is destination.

	A	B	C	D	E
A	0	1	1	1	0
B	0	0	0	0	1
C	0	0	0	1	0
D	0	0	0	0	1
E	0	0	0	0	0

Adjacency list is shown below:

A -> B C D
B -> E
C -> D
D -> E
E ->

9.2: Breadth-First traversal: ABCDE
Depth-First traversal: ABECD
ABEDC
ACDEB
ADEBC
ADECB

9.3: The distance array is shown below:

A	B	C	D	E
0	2	3	10	∞
0	2	3	10	7
0	2	3	5	7
0	2	3	5	6

9.4: (A)

Practice Final Exam

Problem #	Maximal Possible Points	Received
1	6	
2	9	
3	4	
4	12	
5	4	
6	12	
7	3	
8	6	
9	4	
10	3	
11	3	
12	14	
13	20	
Total	100	

*Every problem below has one or more answers. Please select all the correct ones.

Problem #1: For the program below, which one or more of the following are correct?
(A) The output is: 3   5   -5   -3
(B) The output is: 3   5   -3   -5
(C) The output is: 3   5
(D) The output is: 2   4   -4   -2
(E) The output is: 2   4   -2   -4
(F) The output is: 2   4
(G) The output is: 2   4   -3   -5
(H) The output is: 2   4   -5   -3
(I) There is a memory leak in this program.
(J) There is no memory leak in this program.

```cpp
#include <iostream>
#include <vector>
using namespace std;

class myClass
{
public:
    myClass(int v): value( v + 1 )
    {
        cout << v << " ";
    }
    ~myClass()
    {
        cout << -value << " ";
    }
private:
    int value;
};

int main()
{
    vector<myClass*> vec;
    vec.push_back( new myClass(2) );
    vec.push_back( new myClass(4) );
}
```

170

Problem #2: A Fibonacci number is defined as one of a sequence of numbers such that every number is the sum of the previous two numbers except for the first two numbers being 1. Thus, a Fibonacci number is one of: 1 1 2 3 5 8 13 ... etc. Below are two implementations to calculate Fibonacci numbers. Which of the following descriptions are **TRUE**?

(A) Fib(5) = 8
(B) The Big-O complexity of Fib() is O(N)
(C) The Big-O complexity of Fib2() is O(N)
(D) Fib() runs faster than Fib2() when N > 10
(E) Fib2() runs faster than Fib() when N > 10

```cpp
#include <iostream>
using namespace std;

int Fib(int N)
{
    if( N == 0 || N == 1)
        return 1;

    return Fib(N-1) + Fib(N-2);
}

int Fib2(int N)
{
    int *arr = new int[N+1];

    arr[0] = 1;
    arr[1] = 1;
    for(int i = 2; i <= N; i++)
        arr[i] = arr[i-1] + arr[i-2];

    int value = arr[N];

    delete [] arr;

    return value;
}
```

Problem #3: Suppose an array holds a sequence of N unique numbers that are sorted in decreasing order. If we move the last P numbers (P < N) to the beginning of this sequence of numbers, then what is the best possible Big-O time complexity you can achieve to search for a specific given number?
For example, suppose we have the following sequence of numbers:
{ 10 , 9 , 8 , 7 , 6 , 5 , 4 , 3 , 2 , 1 }
Suppose P were 4 and someone moved the last P numbers to the beginning:
{ 4 , 3 , 2 , 1 , 10 , 9 , 8 , 7 , 6 , 5 }
If we don't know P and want to search for a number (say, 7), what is the most efficient algorithm then?

(A) O(N)
(B) O(log N)
(C) O(N log N)
(D) O(1)

Problem #4: Which of the following descriptions are **TRUE** about Linked List?

(A) The Big-O complexity to insert a node into a singly linked list is always O(1).
(B) The Big-O complexity to delete a node from a doubly linked list is always O(1).
(C) If there are both head and tail pointers in doubly linked list, then the insertion and deletion operation is always O(1) at the beginning and end of the list.
(D) If a stack is implemented using a singly linked list, then it is more efficient to use the head pointer as the top of the stack.
(E) If a queue is implemented using a singly linked list (with tail pointer), then it is more efficient to use the tail pointer as the front of the queue and the head pointer as the rear of the queue than vice versa.
(F) Given only a pointer pointing to one of the nodes to be deleted, it is more efficient to delete that node in a doubly linked list than in a singly linked list.
(G) Merging two sorted linked lists, each with N nodes, is O(N).

Problem #5: Which of the following are **TRUE** about Binary Search Trees (BST) with no special attention paid to balancing, and Balanced BSTs?

(A) Search operations are always O(log N) in Binary Search Tree.
(B) The search operation in Binary Search Tree is O(log N) in the worst case.
(C) The insertion operation in Binary Search Tree is O(log N) in the worst case.
(D) The output from in-order traversal on Binary Search Tree is always sorted.
(E) After inserting N keys and deleting a random number of P keys (P < N) in a Binary Search Tree, the resulting Binary Search Tree is always perfectly balanced.
(F) Balanced Search Trees never ensure that all insertion, deletion, and search operations are O(log N).

Problem #6: Given the following insert() operations into an empty Binary Search Tree with no attention paid to balancing. Insert(2), Insert(0), Insert(1), Insert(3), Insert(5), Insert(7), Insert(9). Which of the following are true?

(A) The numbers that the pre-order traversal visited are in this order: 2 0 1 3 5 7 9
(B) The numbers that the in-order traversal visited are in this order: 0 1 2 3 5 7 9
(C) The numbers that the post-order traversal visited are in this order: 1 0 9 5 7 3 2
(D) After Delete(5), the numbers that the post-order traversal visited are in this order: 1 0 9 7 3 2.
(E) After Delete(5), the numbers that the level-order traversal visited are in this order: 2 0 3 1 7 9

Problem #7: Which of the following sorting algorithms is the fastest when applying it to sort this sequence of numbers: {5, 17, 50, 55, 65, 70, 80, 90, 100}?

(A) Quick Sort
(B) Merge Sort
(C) Selection Sort
(D) Insertion Sort
(E) Heap Sort

Problem #8: Which of the followings are **TRUE**?

(A) If there are N numbers in a max heap, finding the 2nd largest number takes no better than O(log N) time.
(B) If there are N numbers in a max heap, using level order traversal on this max heap returns N numbers that are sorted in descending order.
(C) If there are N numbers in a min heap, using level order traversal on this min heap returns N numbers that are sorted in ascending order.
(D) There exists a max heap (with more than 1 node) that is a binary search tree.
(E) If there are N numbers in the array, the Big-O complexity of Heapsort is O(NlogN).

Problem #9: Here is a list of 10 numbers that are partially sorted. Which sorting algorithm(s) could have produced the following array after 2 iterations?
Original sequence: 30,20,40,50,60,10,70,90,80,0
Sequence after 2 iterations: 20 30 40 50 60 10 70 90 80 0

(A) Selection Sort
(B) Insertion Sort
(C) Bubble Sort

173

Problem #10: What is the Big-O complexity of the following function isV2inV1()?
(A) O(N1)
(B) O(N1 + N2)
(C) O(N2)
(D) O(N1*N2)

```cpp
bool isV2inV1(int v1[], int N1,int v2[], int N2)
{
    int i = 0, j = 0;
    while( i < N1 && j < N2 ) {
        if(v1[ i ] == v2[ j ]) {
            i++;
            j++;
        }
        else
            i++;
    }
    if( j == N2)
        return true;
    return false;
}
```

Problem #11: What is the Big-O complexity of the following program?
(A) O(N^2)
(B) O(N^3)
(C) O(N^4)
(D) O(N^5)

```cpp
#include <iostream>
using namespace std;
int main() {
    int N;
    cin >> N;
    for(int i=1; i <= N ; i++)
        for(int j=1; j <= i*i ; j++)
            if(j % i == 0)
                for(int k = 0 ; k < j ; k++ )
                    cout << ".";
            else
                cout << endl;
}
```

```cpp
#include <iostream>
#include <string>
using namespace std;
class Other
{
    int value;
public:
    Other(int n): value(n)          { cout << "O" << value; }
    ~Other()                        { cout << "~O" << value; }
};
class Base
{
public:
    Base(int i):o(i)                { cout << " B "; value = i; }
    virtual ~Base()                 { cout << " ~B "; }
    virtual void output_value()     { cout << value ; }
private:
    int value;
    Other o;
};
class Derived : public Base
{
public:
    Derived(int i): Base(i+1),value(i),o(i)     { cout << " D "; }
    ~Derived()                                  { cout << " ~D "; }
    virtual void output_value()                 { cout << value ; }
private:
    int value;
    Other o;
};

void processAll(Base *bp)
{
    bp->output_value();
    delete bp;
}

int main()
{
    processAll( new Base(2) );      cout << " ";
    processAll( new Derived(3) );   cout << endl;
}
```

175

Problem #13: You have had enough of this weird rainforest and decided to go back to the civilized world. Unfortunately, since you solved the water jug problem last time (see Problem #4 in Practice Midterm II), the cannibals believe that eating you will give them the wisdom you have. Thus, you are now being chased by 300 cannibals. The only way to return to the civilized world is to go through a maze. Fortunately, you stole a map of this maze from one of the cannibals, but you found that this maze is not a common maze. There are many rocks blocking the road here and there. Although you can use a bomb in your bag to smash the rocks to get through, you only have 2 bombs left. Thus, you decided to write a program to figure out whether you are able to use 2 bombs to smash 2 rocks and get to the exit. If so, then print out the moves you need to take in order to get to the exit.

Given the following map (S is the start, Q is the exit, R is a Rock, W is a wall)

```
SWWWWWWWW
..WWWWWWW
W...WWWWW
W.WRWWWWW
..W......W
.WWWRW.WRW
.WWWRW.W.W
RWW..W.RWW
WWWWWW.WRQ
WWWWWW...W
```

Your program should output: (Directions S/E/N/W indicate South/East/North/West)
SESEES Bomb!
SEEESSSSSEEN Bomb!
E Found Exit!

```cpp
#include <iostream>
#include <string>
using namespace std;

int direction[4][2] = { {-1,0}, {0,-1}, {1,0}, {0,1} };
string dir_str[4] = {"N","W","S","E"};

void find_path(char maze[10][11], int bx, int by, int x,int y,
               string path, int numBomb, bool &found );

int main()
{
    char maze[10][11] = {
        "SWWWWWWWWW",
        "..WWWWWWW",
        "W...WWWWWW",
        "W.WRWWWWW",
        "..W......W",
        ".WWWRW.WRW",
        ".WWWRW.W.W",
        "RWW..W.RWW",
        "WWWWWW.WRQ",
        "WWWWWW...W"
    };

    bool found = false;
    string path;
    find_path(maze, 10,11, 0, 0, path, 2, found);
}
```

```cpp
void find_path(char maze[10][11], int bx, int by, int x,int y,
               string path, int numBomb, bool &found )
{
    if(found) return ;

    for(int i=0;i<4;i++)
    {
        int next_x = _____;

        int next_y = _____;

        if( next_x >= 0 && next_y >= 0 && next_x < bx && next_y < by)
        {
            if( maze[ next_x ][ next_y ] == '.' )
            {
                maze[ next_x ][ next_y ] = 'V';

                find_path(maze, bx , by , next_x, next_y,
                        path + dir_str[i] , _____,_____ );

                if ( ! found)
                    maze[ next_x ][ next_y ] = '.';
            }
            else if( _____ && _____ )
            {
                // Smash the rocks with your bomb if you have any.
                maze[ next_x ][ next_y ] = 'V';

                find_path( _____
                        path + dir_str[i] + " Bomb!\n",_____,_____);

                if ( ! found)
                    maze[ next_x ][ next_y ] = _____
            }
            else if(maze[ next_x ][ next_y ] == 'Q')
            {
                path += dir_str[i] + " Found Exit!\n";
                found = true;
                for(int j=0;j<path.size();j++)
                    cout << path[j];
            }
        }
    }
}
// If you can solve this problem, you will return back to the civilized world.
// If not, then …. (BAD END)
```

Practice Final Exam – Solution

1: (F)(I)

2: (A)(C)(E)

3: (B)

The program below gives a binary search algorithm to find the number in O(logN).

```cpp
#include <iostream>
using namespace std;
bool binarySearch(int arr[], int target, int left, int right)
{
    while (left <= right)
    {
        cout << "Left = " << left << ", right = " << right;
        int middle = left + (right - left) / 2;
        cout << ", middle = " << middle << endl;
        if (arr[middle] == target)
            return true;
        if (arr[middle] > arr[right])
        {   // This part (middle to right) is sorted in descending order
            if (arr[middle] > target && target >= arr[right])
                left = middle + 1; // target is in this range
            else
                right = middle; // otherwise it's on the other side
        }
        else
        {   // This part (left to middle) is sorted in descending order
            if (arr[left] >= target && target > arr[middle])
                right = middle - 1;
            else
                left = middle;
        }
    }
    return false;
}
int main()
{
    int N;
    int arr[] = { 4 , 3 , 2 , 1 , 10 , 9 , 8 , 7 , 6 , 5 };

    cin >> N;
    bool found = binarySearch(arr, N, 0, 9);
    if (found)
        cout << "Found " << N << "!" << endl;
}
```

4: (C)(D)(F)(G)

5: (D)

6: (A)(B)(D)(E)

7: (D)

8: (D)(E)

9: (B)

10: (A)

11: (C)

This if statement, if (j % i == 0), only is true when j is a multiple of i. In other words, only when j = 1*i, 2*i, 3*i, ... , (i)(i) will the if (j % i == 0) is true. So when i is equal to N, this j-loop + if-statement is true N times.

The else part (cout << endl;) is true $N^2 - N$ times.

```
for(int i=1 ; i <= N ; i++)                    <= O(N)
    for(int j=1; j <= i*i ; j++)
        if(j % i == 0)                         <= O(i) = O(N)
            for(int k = 0 ; k < j ; k++ )      <= O(N^2)
                cout << ".";
        else
            cout << endl;                      <= O(i^2 - i) = O(N^2 - N)
```

Thus, the overall complexity is:
$$O(N * ((N * N^2) + (N^2 - N))) = O(N^4 + N^3 - N^2) = O(N^4)$$

12: O2 B 2 ~B ~O2 O4 B O3 D 3 ~D ~O3 ~B ~O4

13: The find_path function can be implemented as:

```cpp
void find_path(char maze[10][11], int bx, int by, int x, int y,
    string path, int numBomb, bool &found)
{
    if (found) return;
    for (int i = 0; i<4; i++) {
        int next_x = x + direction[i][0];
        int next_y = y + direction[i][1];
        if (next_x >= 0 && next_y >= 0 && next_x < bx && next_y < by) {
            if (maze[next_x][next_y] == '.') {
                maze[next_x][next_y] = 'V';
                find_path(maze, bx, by, next_x, next_y,
                    path + dir_str[i], numBomb, found);
                if (!found)
                    maze[next_x][next_y] = '.';
            }
            else if (maze[next_x][next_y] == 'R' && numBomb > 0) {
                // Smash the rocks with your bomb if you have any.
                maze[next_x][next_y] = 'V';
                find_path(maze, bx, by, next_x, next_y,
                    path + dir_str[i] + " Bomb!\n", numBomb - 1, found);
                if (!found)
                    maze[next_x][next_y] = 'R';
            }
            else if (maze[next_x][next_y] == 'Q') {
                path += dir_str[i] + " Found Exit!\n";
                found = true;
                for (int j = 0; j<path.size(); j++)
                    cout << path[j];
            }
        }
    }
}
```